10

D

EXPERIENCE IN ACTION

A
Psychomotor
Psychology

by Albert Pesso

New York: New York University Press
1973

To My Father
Yakov Bohor Saba Ben Pinhas Pesso
1895-1972

Library of Congress Catalog Card Number: 72-96481
ISBN: 0-8147-6559-9

Preface

The time of this writing represents the completion of ten years of practice and growth in psychomotor therapy. The completion of my first book marked three years of learning in this process. This writing, therefore, is the fruit of the past three years plus an overview and clarification of all that went on before.

During this time I have had the opportunity to work with hundreds of people in groups and in individual sessions; I have learned how to train others to do psychomotor therapy and how to profit from that experience in teaching another generation of psychomotor therapists. Much new knowledge has come from the experience of teaching and lecture giving. The questions that have arisen regarding the differences between traditional psychotherapy and psychomotor therapy have naturally led to the exploration of answers. The questions are still generating answers in my mind and this present writing will perhaps be a thinking aloud and further clarification of the differences and similarities, as well as an attempt to build a language bridge between the two modes of thinking and working.

Throughout this period I have not been a passive observer/documenter. As well as a therapist/teacher, I have been an active participant/group member. I have been deeply moved in many sessions and I have learned to look at the role of the therapist through the eyes of a real responding, feeling human being. The relationship between therapist and client has been developed differently in psychomotor therapy sessions than in traditional group therapy sessions, perhaps due to the different mode that is used and perhaps due to the personal make-up of the founders of this therapy—my wife, Diane, and myself. Nonetheless, psychomotor therapy has developed a world view and behavioral modes and attitudes which I feel are valuable and worth presenting.

The basic questions—what is life? What are man's function and role in life? What is a mature man? How does one live in reality with some measure of equanimity and joy—are responded to differently as a result of experience in psychomotor therapy. I would like to spend some time with those philosophical questions and examine the theoretical concepts and the practices that have led to attempts at answers. I hope to highlight that inquiry with specific case studies which will show how such concepts were arrived at.

CONTENTS

CHAPTER I

What is Life?

Life comes from life. Life needs and relates to life. Life flows into life. Life flows out of life. Life makes shapes and forms which determine how these processes will come about. Life is simple and complex. Sometimes the greatest simplicity is effected by complex means; sometimes the greatest complexity is effected by simple means.

Life is not static, but active. Life needs energy in order to live. The energy is used to grow and sustain itself to move with, and to sense or know. Life is born, lives, and dies on the individual level and on the specie level, creating developmental rhythms. Life on the plant level seems constantly to articulate itself toward greater and more complex action, sensing, and knowing, with a rhythm that includes being born and developing itself but not yet the process of dying. Yet surely other planets, in other solar systems, have given birth to life, have seen it flourish, and then die.

The stages of an individual life include being born, the establishment and clarification of modes of relationship to that from which it is born and to other like-born things; development of methods by which one takes energy from other life systems; separation from and clarification in relation to other life systems; development of the capacity to produce energy and life; relating to those life systems one produces; separation from the life one produces; death and decay.

Consider a tree. It is born as a seed. As a seed it is made up of material of the parent tree and is indeed literally part of the parent tree. At some point in its development the seed is disengaged from the parent tree and becomes itself a total separate entity. The seed then creates an energy relationship with the soil it falls in and the sun and water which, it is to be hoped, will be present. Roots in the ground take in the energy of soil nutrients, and leaves above ground take in the energy of the sun. Both these energies are applied to the process of becoming a seedling and then a sapling.

In effect the plant is in relationship with other species of plant which chemically dictate what shall and what shall not grow in the soil near where they are. The chemistry of the soil may be such that the leaves of other species or even its own species might inhibit it from growing.

Gravity plays a part in the perpendicularity of the trunk and the relationship of the cells to one another. The tree takes in energy and converts it into leaves, chemicals, and wood. At some point in its growth the young tree begins to produce materials for seed, and those seeds in turn fall away and produce other young trees. Eventually the young tree grows large, if all goes well, and its leaves and shadow dictate to all vegetation in the near vicinity how much it can grow.

After years of seed production, the tree, having accumulated the scars of time and aging, is no longer able to process the energy of the sun and the earth, and its living system halts. Nonetheless its energy passes to other forms of life, possibly as compost or fire, but no longer in an interchanging and stable way. This dying, decaying energy process demands that it no longer be a tree but be reduced to its less complex elements. Unless transplanted, it is still in the same place in which it took root, and, although having gone through several stages, it is still a tree of its species. When its active participation in the energy-transference process ends, it loses its complex and interactive structure as well as its store of energy and control of its processes; it is then consumed in some way by the environment or by other living systems.

Somehow life manages an ecological balance of inner energies and outer energies that permits a dynamic stability during the lifetime of a living organism. A single life does not and cannot live in a vacuum. Other life entities of similar and different form are necessary for the continuity of the individual life. All life forms must keep the bulk of their energy system within, and enclosed, and must have sensory and control mechanisms attached to them which manage the energy flow appropriately. The energy of the sun does not enter the tree just anywhere on the surface of the tree but specifically on the surface of its leaves. The sun, so to speak, bounces off the trunk and the branches and the twigs. The rain and dissolved nutrients of the soil do not enter the tree through the trunk or the leaves but are literally shed by all parts of the tree except its root system which is prepared to process them.

The living processes of the tree and of all life are designed with specific functions, with little interchangeability. The tree is also so structured as to function within a certain quantitative range of sunlight and water supply. Should there be too much of either, the organization of the tree would break down. Each species of tree being nicely adapted to its climate belt, this rarely happens except for the interventions of man or dramatic changes in the environment such as floods, droughts, etc.

It is a function of life to produce more life and, over long periods of time, more adaptable and more conscious life. Sometimes the life force struggles to maintain itself and sometimes it seems to be engrossed in a dance of itself and within itself for no other reason than to dance the dance of living things. Life is a living possibility which seems to be its own reason for existence. Were we to have choice as infants, knowing the pain as well as the joys of life, knowing what was to be lived through before inevitable death, would we choose to be born? The quality of the life envisaged would tend to influence the answer.

On Being Human

We have the curious privilege of being both alive and human. Human life is very different from other forms of life in that we have so much more consciousness and so much more choice available to us than have other forms. Not that our lives consist entirely of consciousness and choice, but that the quality of our lives can be considerably affected and altered by the knowing and choosing that we do.

Consciousness and choice are not thrust on us the instant we emerge from the womb. Is a baby conscious? Does it make choices? Certainly, but not to the extent that an adult does. Indeed that is one of the problems of becoming an adult, learning the range and limits of those abilities, as well as all the other capabilities a human inherits.

A tree is not very flexible. It cannot move, it is not conscious, it does not seem to make any choices yet it lives its treeness successfully. Humans are so flexible in comparison. We can move, can know, can choose, can adapt. We are not frozen to our environment nor to our innate structure. However we cannot ignore the fact that we do have an innate structure that has been passed down to us from the beginning of time. This structure, though we are not conscious of it (or possibly even it of us), knows and recognizes life as all life forms know and recognize life, and stubbornly clings to its patterns of survival. I do not believe that we can become conscious of all that we are and be able to choose all we can be or will be; but we must come to terms with those forces and powers within us, over which we will never have control, in order to make of the total of ourselves a harmonious entity. Such an entity fits in with all the natural world of unconscious, partly conscious, and wholly conscious life that includes our human adaptability and learning capacities. The humanness should and can be used to enhance and focus what is native to us and all life. Humanness is not against nature nor above nature, but is an outgrowth of nature. Like a powerful focusing lens, our human capacities should intensify life and bring it to its highest clarity, consciousness, and innate capacity for fulfillment.

Being human is more than just being alive. Each leaf of a tree is part of a pattern that one can discern when one looks at a tree from a distance. The leaf, though, does not "know" it is part of a pattern and does not "know" the shape of the tree nor choose to be part of it. The individual leaf, as well as the individual tree, has an identity, a place, and a function without knowing it. A human has the capacity to know his position relative to other humans and the ability to alter it, deny it, shape it in such a way as to enhance the group or himself, ignore it, or accept it.

When a child is born to a family it is analogous to a leaf being born to a branch. By virtue of its position within the family, certain behaviors will be expected of it, certain responsibilities will be thrust upon it, certain events will assert themselves in relation to it. In short, the power of external demands and events will be quite strong in pressuring it to a predestined place, much as the leaf is predestined by its inner nature and force of external nature to take its unconscious place. How much can man, by the use and force of his ability to know and choose, safely—for himself and for his immediate family and the family of man—alter his position in the family? How radically can he change and still maintain his sanity and capacity to have pleasure and to function?

If knowing and choosing were considered God's right and not man's right, could man become a full human being by our definition? Certainly some cultures restrict knowing. Perhaps not all knowing but some knowing is seen as God's province and other knowing as man's. Consider the fate of Adam and Eve who learned to know good and evil. In the Biblical myth they were banished literally from the world of earthly and unconscious pleasure. Is the lesson here that it is better not to know and stay happy or that it is all right to know but that you will lose your capacity for pleasure and joy if you do? Do knowing and choosing inevitably lead to suffering and severance from the natural world of beauty and bliss? Does knowing separate man from nature or is his knowing a tool of nature to improve on itself? Is the point of education and therapy to create and develop suffering, intelligent stoics—incapable of spontaneity and joy?

Clearly, educators and therapists should have a world view and frame of reference within which their work can be understood. What are the goals of therapy and education—therapy to heal the sick human and bring him back to life and humanness? Education to lead the normal human to the fulfillment of his life and humanness? But what do we mean by *life* and *humanness?* I will attempt to define, to the best of my ability, what I mean by those terms as well as the terms *therapy* and *education.* I hope to present a unified theory and approach in the use of psychomotor techniques for educational and therapeutic ends that will be consistent with a world view of man's life and his humanness that would seem to permit him the greatest knowing, choosing, sensing, feeling, thinking, acting, and joy that he is capable of, while enhancing the lives of those around him and in the rest of the world.

CHAPTER 2

Psychomotor Sessions as an Arena
for Learning
for the Therapist and Client

Psychomotor therapy sessions* have afforded me a valuable classroom for the observation of emotional phenomena and behavior. Sessions include "structures" during which a group member reexperiences memories and feelings, and, in addition, permits the tensions and bodily changes felt during these "structures" to be the impetus for action. The client is encouraged to move in any way that the body tensions seem to call forth. For instance, if the tension is felt in the hand, he is encouraged to move his hand in any way that would either reduce the tension or "use" the tension. The aim is not to make the tension "go away" as one wishes an unpleasant feeling to go away, but to move in the direction of the tension, thus permitting it to become overt action.

The psychomotor process is based on the hypothesis that emotions tend to become action and action seeks to find appropriate or satisfying interactions. Psychomotor group members are taught to become sensitive to the relationship between emotions and action so that they can begin to move directly to the impulses they discover in their bodies. They are also taught accommodation, which is a way of controlling the interaction process to provide satisfaction to the action that is expressed. In the energy—action—interaction hypothesis the accommodation or controlled interaction is seen to "match" the action that is being expressed, in the way one part of a jigsaw puzzle

---

* See Albert Pesso, *Movement in Psychotherapy*. New York: New York University Press, 1969

7

matches or fits into another part. It is understood in psychomotor theory that many emotions are not experienced or actions expressed by people because the family setting or circumstances they were raised in did not provide satisfactory accommodation or "matching" responses to their feelings or behaviors. By offering accommodation to as yet unexpressed emotions and behaviors, the psychomotor process taps the reservoir of repressed, inhibited and unconscious feelings and permits those aspects of one's being that have yet to be discovered, to be expressed and hopefully, to be integrated into one's life.

The specific process in a psychomotor group in which this takes place is called a *structure*. In a structure one group member at a time is given twenty-five minutes during which he explores his own personal feeling state and develops out of that an interpersonal relationship using other group members as accommodators. When a person in a structure expresses anger, by punching, biting, or kicking, the accommodation includes actions and sounds that simulate the responses to punching, etc. The satisfactory accommodation of anger includes the death or destruction of the target figure. To offset the loss of important figures in a structure, the psychomotor process offers *polarized,* or two sets of, figures. A group member is offered a negative mother and father and a positive mother and father. The negative figures represent only the negative aspects of the real-life, many faceted figures. When they are symbolically destroyed it is not as if one is killing one's *entire* parents. The positive parental figures do not represent the positive aspects of the real figures but idealized or archetypical parents who perfectly satisfy the needs for growth. A structure provides an opportunity for symbolic re-birth in a perfect setting that matches his need for expression and personal growth. In psychomotor theory the major developmental needs that must be met are nurturance, support, protection, and limits. The positive parent figures fill the deficits of one's real or fantasied past. It is postulated that when developmental needs are met the further process of becoming one's uniquely creative self can be attended to with more energy and less distraction.

This matching of action and response gives us a picture of what the ideal childhood would be like as seen from the viewpoint of a remembering, feeling adult. It also permits a testing of behaviors and responses. One may think that he wishes to perform a certain action to correspond to a certain feeling or tension, but when he actually makes that movement he may find that it is not at all what he thought it would be, and that he has done it without any strong feeling or impetus. It is possible that one could be denying that feeling and therefore have no emotion attached to the expression of it; but if the client has worked for some time, those feelings and behaviors that are possible for him to express with emotion come out sharply and clearly.

When a client considers what responses he wants from his accommodators, he may request a response that seems satisfying to him in his mind, but when he experiences it it may seem bland or unpleasant or unwanted. When he asks the accommodator to respond in other ways, he may find exactly the response that suits him or that has been waiting for without perhaps knowing that he has been waiting for it. The same is true of his own behavior. When he moves in the way that his body would seem to indicate, the satisfying or matching response is unmistakable.

It is by watching the congruency between feeling, action, and response in thousands of hours of structures that I have felt that a pattern of interaction for different ages of life can be discerned. It has seemed to me that certain predictable things occur or should occur in infancy, in childhood, and in adolescence that permit emotional growth. Observation of clients of different ages, from ten through seventy, and of different backgrounds and cultures has led to the belief that there are some universal "givens" that must be met in terms of action and response, which permit the cultivation of the most consciousness and choice while maintaining individual cohesion and remaining alive in the fullest sense.

Conflict Between Cultural Background and What is Learned in Therapy

It is conceivable that psychomotor therapy could put a client in conflict with his religion or culture; hence it is the job of the therapist to work with this person in such a way that the models of behavior that are extended and permitted do not jeopardize his standing in his cultural community. It is also conceivable that the client considers his inherited culture to be alien to his "true" nature, and psychomotor therapy could be used to assist him in finding the "rest" of himself that his culture has not evoked and help him locate his place in the world at large.

Another alternative would be to assist a person in becoming himself and then aid him in finding or translating those tenets of his culture that support that growth. Often one can work with an individual who feels that he must rebel against his family or his culture for he feels that they are his enemies and that they will "kill" him. He may find that those very things he was rebelling against can be usefully integrated into his world view and his self-concept.

Toward a Universal Culture

Although there are aspects of psychomotor therapy that would seem to lead toward the development of a universal culture regarding man's emotional and behavioral self, its over-all aim is toward inclusiveness rather than exclusiveness. That is, it is directed to accepting and including all that man is and can be, rather than limiting and defining narrowly only those things that permit man to be called man.

Acting Versus Thinking in Learning about Emotional Desires

This manner of learning about man's nature by watching people in their structures highlights the important difference between a man "thinking and saying" and one "experiencing and doing." I or one of my clients might "think or say" that such and such a behavioral response would be the ideal or most appropriate for a given emotional memory or circumstance, but it is only by the client's actually "experiencing" his accomodator's responses and "doing" his own emotional movement that he and I both learn what his emotional, motoric, bodily (instinctual, if you will) requisites are.

What Does the Young Human Organism Need?

From a combination of reading, speculation and watching clients during structures being born or in which they reexperience intrauterine existence, this picture results.

When the organism is conceived, it is made up of material from two individuals. It is not itself yet. It is not aware of itself as a separate entity. It requires that the materials from the two parents have sufficient compatibility and genetic content to effect the conception and keep the life process developing. It needs to find, or be placed, or fall upon the appropriate place on the uterine wall (somewhat as the seed of a tree has to find, or be placed, or fall upon fertile ground), and that wall and the materials around it must be compatible with the new organism. Apparently if any of the foregoing conditions are not present, or if the materials are in any way defective, a natural abortion takes place.

If all goes well, it could be said that the sperm "knows" how to find the egg, that both sperm and egg "know" how to unite, that the new organism "knows" how to find the appropriate place on the uterine wall, and that the wall "knows" how to relate appropriately to the growing organism.

What Can We Learn from This?

I would like to explore the area of human psychic structure and also of memory. It is a real event that we talk about when we speak of the sperm and egg coming together to form one organism. That means that at the deepest roots of our structure, we were at one time two and not one. Is there some primitive memory of this twoness and does this twoness pervade or influence our nervous system?

Recent experiments have shown that a foetus can be conditioned in utero. How far back can we go and find learning and memory possibilities? Can an egg learn? Can a sperm learn? Can they remember? Do they bring their remembered history together? How and when do the two systems unite to become one and experience themselves as one? Is not this oneness—to unify under one banner all that one is—becoming the entire point of therapy and education? There is a conscious knowing and an unconscious "knowing." Isn't the job of therapy to bring these two knowings together?

If there are memory traces from our earliest prenatal selves, it seems likely to me that they would reside not in our conscious minds, which did not yet exist, but in our organisms or "body-minds." This seeking of "data" from our "body-minds," and bringing them to an arena where all the learning and information stored in our parental genes can be reaped, is the central principle of psychomotor therapy.

It is commonplace that individuals under stress seem to regress to an earlier, less complex, more satisfying past. Sometimes clients, from normal to psychotic, may find themselves during a structure in foetal position and wish to be covered over completely and to feel the pressure of people's bodies or hands, or of pillows around them. This is quite different from a nurturance structure where the client wishes to be held and nurse in the arms of the mother, with the arms of the father embracing the two of them to give them support and protection. The latter structure indicates a higher level of trust.

Trusting Life

The foetal structure connotes a return to a different order of trusting or not trusting. The client in the foetal structure may verbalize his feeling that his parents didn't know how to take care of him. He may say that living is too painful and impossible; that he doesn't know how to live; that his parents never saw, understood or responded to him; that the world is too crazy, unsafe, and upset to live in; that his parents never wanted him, etc. Obviously this client is not about to trust people. However, he may be able to trust certain natural processes. He can be told that his mother's uterus "knew" him and "understood" him and "responded" to him. He can be told that life is possible, that life does "happen," that even though his parents didn't know how to live themselves nor how to raise him, his innate living material does know how to live and his parents' physiological processes can be trusted.

It is not sufficient simply to tell a client this. He must also experience the warmth and safety of the foetal position. From the warmth of the therapist and other members of the group he may learn to begin to trust people, but first he must find some fundamental process that makes life not only possible, but also relaxing and pleasurable. If he can grasp the experience of the well-cared-for foetus, he can perhaps find a basis on which to go on living, and then can learn to trust people and become a person himself, rather than an unconscious carrier of the life forces within him. Many "normals" can live without trusting others. Somehow they manage to maintain an existence, albeit limited in satisfactions, that can pass in some cultures for the average. Seriously ill persons, however, reach a point where their very existence becomes untenable due to their paucity of conscious or unconscious life experiences that meet even their most meager needs. The rebirth structure offers a possible beginning point for therapy for all those clients who can no longer trust others to any extent to care for their painful lives and who need something beyond people to begin living with.

Another bit of information that can be gathered from the description of conception and the attachment to the uterine wall is the similarity between primitive "knowing" and what is called accommodation in psychomotor therapy. When the sperm can be said to "know" the egg, it can be understood that each has surfaces which permit a mutually satisfying relationship. (In the act of accommodation the satisfaction may not be mutual, but as the accommodator behaves synchronously with the client, the client's satisfaction is high.) When it is said that the uterine wall "knows" or "recognizes" the new organism, it can be understood that it has processes on its surface which match processes on the organism, and that through those processes a relationship occurs which is mutually satisfying, or to put it more simply, a relationship occurs which furthers the development and survival of both sides and therefore has value.

The accommodator, by his very act of synchronous relating, lets the client experience being known and related to. To go back once more to the uterine wall and the implanted organism, there is a further stage which includes the flow of energy in a simple, concrete, and utterly real way. Energy in the form of nurturant fluids does pass between the uterus and the foetus. This represents to me primal knowing, relating, and growing. Whatever is needed by the growing foetus is provided by the uterus, unquestioningly and perfectly. It has led those of us engaged in psychomotor therapy to believe in the intrinsic right of living things to be provided for by the very act of being conceived. There is nothing a fertilized egg must produce or perform. It has an intrinsic right to live by virtue of its being itself. It has an intrinsic right to be provided for by virtue of its being itself. Those clients who feel that they cannot live because they have done nothing worthwhile, or who have performed badly or who have failed, can be reminded that life itself in its most primitive form makes no such demands. It is only later at the more complex level of interaction with one's parents and one's environment that survival depends on performance.

If one were to extend the word *knowing* to include the meanings in *learning*, one could see that in the act of relating (in this basic sense of the word *relating*) one is learning. Accommodation then, which enhances and perfects relating, can be understood as a powerful learning device. The major process by which life goes on can be seen to include the sequence of being, with articulated surfaces which permit relating, and that relating includes the flow of energy, or nurturants, or learning, which permits growth and development. Psychomotor therapy gains its usefulness, I think, from the use in structures of accommodation, which permits this flow to occur in a developmental way.

The basic tool in psychoanalytic therapy is the phenomenon of transference. Transference in psychomotor terms would seem to include the client's expectation of certain relating surfaces or modes from the therapist. When the client in psychotherapy begins to transfer on his therapist, he is in a position to relate and therefore to grow and learn from his relationship. The use of the transference in traditional phenomenon psychotherapy is limited, I think, by the therapist's inability in a one-to-one relationship to accommodate in the psychomotor sense to the client. With the addition of accommodation and the splitting of the target figures in a structure to positive and negative, the therapist is in a position to offer the client the appropriate responses he is anticipating. The traditional therapist does not accommodate either positively or negatively and the learning comes more from what the therapist does not do than from what he does. With accommodation, both positive and negative, the relationships with the therapist as well as with the rest of the group are strongly enhanced. With those relationships and the kinds of controls that exist in psychomotor therapy, the transference can be not only intensified on some levels (in that the flow can go both from client to therapist and from therapist and other group members to client), but diluted on others (by taking the intensity and ambiguity from the therapist and spreading them among the rest of the group).

It seems to me that by not responding in the transference relationship, the therapist is behaving like a uterine wall who says, "I see what it is that you want from me; I hope you see what it is you want from me and understand the fallacy and foolishness of ever expecting me to respond to you as you wish." I admit to overstating the case. It is a rare analytic therapist that would behave in such a passive and then painful manner, but the theory of a Blank Screen does permit the possibility. The psychomotor therapist could provide a different set of responses from those described above. Certainly he would not say that he, personally, was a uterine wall and that he, personally, could provide the necessary nurturant flow. If he did it would make him seem to the client a personal god who could magically save his life. It is important that the psychomotor therapist assist the client in developing a mental or memory set that will place the interaction in the appropriate setting and time. Those group figures who placed pillows, blankets, and their own bodies around the client in the earlier example could represent symbolically the uterine wall, and some female group member's hand, possibly placed against the stomach over the navel, could represent the umbilical cord. The therapist could suggest to the client that he imagine being an embryo and permit himself to fantasize how it would feel to have all this happening to him. The therapist would point out that the client was indeed not now an embryo in fact, but that he could suspend momentarily his adult concept of himself and enjoy the symbolic and fantasized experience of intrauterine living.

All this could be done entirely in fantasy, but it is important to include concrete sensory and motoric input to the fantasy to make it a more believable and educational experience.

Earliest learnings seem to benefit greatly from sensory-motor elements. It is only after such basic concrete events that one can go confidently on to more abstract types of learning and have them be experienced as real. Perhaps those patients who experience little of life as real can be seen to be suffering from lack of satisfying concrete relationships in the earliest days, months, or years. This would point to the value of psychomotor therapy or some other form of therapy using sensory-motor techniques with seriously ill, hospitalized patients.

Memory

What could be the point of a grown individual's going through a structure about being a foetus in a pillow-blanket uterus? What therapeutic use could it have? What educational use could it have? An adult is certainly not an infant. Being an infant is certainly not the problem of that adult. Why not concentrate on what his problems actually are, rather than delve so far back into an uncertainly remembered and probably highly fantasized past?

The question could be responded to by another question, "How does the past, whether remembered or fantasized, affect the present?" What indeed is a memory? Why are some memories so powerful and vivid and some memories so weak? What is the difference between memory and learning, that is, what is the difference between remembering and knowing? Knowing, as we have used it heretofore, presupposes a present, ongoing relationship, or energy interchange, as that between the embryo and the uterine wall. Let us take the meaning behind *memory* apart and see what it consists of. Memory develops from this energy interchange, the effects of which are recorded. The constantly developing embryo is at any given moment the embodiment of all changes produced by the energy interchange. The present, then, is a record of the past, and learning or knowing presupposes change.

All that the new organism is when it begins its existence is a most encapsulated history of its biological past. It carries into its future (by means of its genes) all the knowledge regarding living itself that has been accumulated by the race without the excess baggage of memory of the specific events experienced by each individual member of the species. Dying may become a necessity because of the wastefulness of the organism's having so much of its energy wrapped up in recording and recalling so many events. The only way an individual could become immortal would be for him to give up the personal baggage consisting of the record of his personal events and that would be the same as being reborn as one could not (without such record) recall in any way what he had been or been through. However, the recording process takes place in the living cells themselves, so how is one to give that up to begin anew without dying? Death of the individual is the only answer, and perpetuating an abbreviated history of the species the only way to begin again. Perhaps the explanation of the varying longevity of different species lies in their varying capacity to carry history through the present into the future. Death is the price of having a history, or it could even be said that death is the price of life.

How Are Events Recorded?

I should like to explore the old categories of mineral, vegetable, and animal with regard to the recording of events. For mineral, let us take a rock; for vegetable, let us return to our tree; for animal, let us take first a household pet, a cat, and then, separately from the rest of the animal kingdom let us take man.

First, we shall take the rock. The rock, in its immediate present, is the history of all its components. It has within it a record of geological events, including massive heating, congealing, and cooling (not to mention its molecular history in being born in the furnace of the stars). Its particular shape is a record of its interaction with other rocks, with the sun, with ice, with the air. Each interaction with another energy system leaves its mark or its record on the very structure of the rock. The rock remains a rock, recording the events that bespeak its energy interactions from the past into the present, so long as energy that reaches it is no greater than its intrinsic energy to maintain its shape or coherence. For example, if that rock were at the seashore, it might record the interaction with the sun, with the air, with the water, and with other rocks and grains of sand that have been washed over it. The smoothness or roundness of the rock would attest to or record the energy interaction with the sand and water; the chemistry of its surface would attest to the energy interaction with the sun's rays. Should a larger and heavier rock fall on our rock with a certain momentum, our rock might split and no longer be itself. Should the sun's rays or the heat of the sand or air become such that they would melt the components of the rock, it would no longer be itself. Should the air or the sun or the water, over a period of time, strip away all the particles of the rock, molecule by molecule, the rock would no longer be itself.

The rock, then, maintains its identity only so long as the energy of its interactive events is not greater than the energy of its coherence. This would hold true for the vegetable and animal kingdoms as well. There is a range, therefore, within which learning, knowing, relating, and recording can take place, but beyond which dissolution and death of the individual result. That is, if one is to control the length of one's life, one has to have some control over the energy of interactive events. But what is a rock to do? Can a rock say, following an impact with a medium-sized rock which duly left its mark in the form of a chipped edge on our rock, "Boy, that was a close one. I'd better look out for medium-sized rocks in this vicinity"? First of all, can a rock sense its vicinity, as well as sense the shape of other-sized rocks, and even if it did, what could it do to alter the course of events? Could it respond differently to the course of events, or tell other rocks—that it knew and liked—how to deal with medium-sized, edge-chipping rocks? All our poor rock can do is record the impact and "know" about medium-sized rocks, in an even less "knowing" way than the seed "knew" the earth, the water, and the sunshine.

The seed arrives on the earth packed with history, but in a different way than does the rock. First of all, the seed is alive, which basically means that it has the capacity to reproduce itself. The history it carries is not its own individual history, for truly it hardly has one, but the history of the species. The seed "knows" (remembers?) how to interact with the elements so as to become a tree that can produce seeds that know how to become trees. At this point perhaps we should clarify the use of the word *know*. It seems necessary to divide "knowing" into three aspects of one process: knowing as interrelating; knowing as learning; and knowing as remembering or recalling. Having a history of successful living is valuable to the seed, for should it find the same conditions in its own present that permitted trees to exist in the past, it can bring this information successfully to bear upon the interactive events in the environment. In other words, having a genetic memory makes the future possible so long as the future is very much like the past. If there were sudden or rapid changes in the environment, the seed would have no chance, but with the operation of natural selection and with slow environmental changes, it could "learn" new things with which to cope with the changes. In a sense the seed which becomes a tree has a past and a present but really very little future. Individually, it cannot plan or prepare for changes that may be forthcoming in a way that a human can. In a certain sense the tree making a seed is "experiencing" the future. It would be a more accurate experiencing of or preparing for the future if its seeds were different from what it was as a seed.

To sum up: the tree's memory is genetic. A tree's individual history of having experienced small changes in the environment is not what it recalls in order to cope with these changes the next time they occur. For instance, consider the small environmental change of the earth's rotation, causing the sun to be at different angles and directions in relation to the tree at different times. The tree doesn't change its leaf angles because it remembers that that is what happened yesterday, but its genetic make-up is such that the action of the sunlight causes cells to grow in such a way as to cause the leaves to face in different directions. The tree can be said to be knowing, or relating to, the apparent movement of the sun, but it is only learning the same lesson that all trees of its species can learn. Its response is not a new learning, but the repetition of an old lesson. Let us not derogate old lessons, however, for they make tree survival possible.

Let us take note of another factor. When the position of the sun changes, sensory mechanisms in the structure of the branch and twig, which measure the amount of sunlight, release or inhibit the growth-producing substances in the appropriate places to bring about the necessary angle changes. This can be seen as a primitive stimulus-response mechanism. What I mean to illustrate is the hookup between sensory mechanisms and behavior-modifying mechanisms in nature, even including the vegetable kingdom. Trees, as with all living things, must have methods of controlling the energy interactions with the environment, as stated earlier, in order to maintain a dynamic equilibrium. The control of the energy can come about from the structure of the tree (bark, roots, branches, etc.) as well as from the cellular response of the tree. Indeed the greatest control factors in the tree are in its structure, as noted previously.

Clearly, genetic memory or knowing is crucial for survival of the species, if not always of the individual. As one goes up the scale of living things, one realizes that upon genetic memory and knowing is built the possibility of individual memory and knowing. Interestingly, there is a corresponding lessening of numbers of seeds or new infants as life becomes more conscious and individualized. Let us now examine the animal kingdom with the household cat as our subject. In addition to considering the meaning and value of memory in respect to the control of the environment and of the future for the species and the individual, we are even more concerned with the value of memory in therapy. The cat has genetic memory, as is evidenced by its structure and behavior. The cat looks and acts like a cat. That is, she (I refer to my black female mother cat) moves and behaves in certain situations much like any other member of her species. She is certainly herself as an individual. She is recognizably herself, much as a tree is individually recognizable as itself. The cat's and the tree's individual histories of interactions are each uniquely their own as no other cat and no other tree lives in precisely their time and space.

The genetic memory of the cat family shows up very strongly in the mating season. A neighbor's male cat showed up on our back deck for many days courting our female. The male knew we had a female, and, when he had the chance, knew how to relate to her sexually for very soon our black cat was pregnant. I should describe something of the appearance, behavior, and attitude of the neighbor cat when he waited for our black cat to make herself available. We have an opening onto our deck which has large glass sliding doors. When the drapes were open in the evening we could see the neighbor cat staring intently inside while he yowled loudly. Should our black cat be visible, his interest would seem to increase and he would seem to be looking for some way to get beyond the glass door. If we decided to let our black cat out at these times, if she was so inclined, he would move rapidly to her and show even more heightened interest. It seemed to me that our lovers were in this state for at least a few weeks and possibly a month. (Perhaps it is just the attitude of parents of a daughter, but that neighbor cat seemed to be endlessly hanging around the house and was a perfect nuisance.) The one or two times I came upon the pair actually engaged in sexual intercourse they seemed entirely engrossed, full of energy and excitement and of course behaving exactly and in the same position, including male's vise-like hold with his jaws on the female's neck and head, as all cats probably have through history. But those cats were not bored! They were obviously living spontaneously in the moment. They were very likely experiencing powerful emotional sensations; and if we could monitor their bloodstreams, we would find a veritable storm of hormones. But those cats were not just the blind, mechanical, abused pawns of nature; they were nature itself in the bodies of cats having a ball! If Zen teaches us to seek and find eternity in the mundane, they were well taught! If our hippie youth teach us to "swing" and "go with it," those cats know all about it.

This raises the question: How much free will is there, if any, in the natural world? There is clear evidence of individuality and uniqueness, but is there free will? More specifically, what evidence is there of free will in the human and what do education and/or therapy do toward developing that capacity? Or is the goal of education and therapy the grateful and humble acceptance of the world as it is—that is, adjustment? Without choice, what changes can education and/or therapy actually bring about? What is the range and limit of changes, assuming that change is a possibility? These are interesting questions. Where is free will in this case for the cats? What would the point of free will be in this case? If those cats were human they could choose many, many alternatives of behavior, but which would cause the most joy? If they were brought up in certain religions, they could perhaps decide not to have intercourse and experience instead the joy of renunciation. Or, and this is an important point, they could consciously know as humans that they were being deeply influenced in their feelings and behavior by their genes, and consciously and freely decide to let themselves be excited and moved by those feelings and drives. Is that a legitimate use of the term *free will?*

There would have to be important differences, of course, between the cats' giving free rein to their instincts and the humans' doing the same. When nature called, the cats were still on our back deck. Should a human pair have remained on the back deck or have found a "more suitable" place? A lot would depend on the background of the lovers and that of those in the house and here we begin to see some of the dilemma of being human. The human knows too much about the implication of his actions and can fall into the human trap of not acting at all.

Cats do not have much range of adaptation for their behavior. But certainly they can learn about their environment and learn how to get the most out of it. Let us see how memory or past experience influences their control of the environment and of the future. We have seen how genetic memory influences the cat's behavior in reproduction, yet there is a more subtle way in which learning that includes genetic memory can take place. Let us say that our pregnant cat has now given birth to her first litter. One of the results of the delivery is that the mother cat begins to have milk at its little teats. The mother cat and the kittens have drives which are mutually satisfying. It does not seem to me that the mother's drive to lie and be suckled and the kittens' drive to suckle are entirely automatic, however; when they find each other doing mutually satisfying things, the obvious pleasure they experience is sure to intensify their actions. They may then learn to perform those actions even better than they could by the influence of their genes alone. What I am outlining is the relationship between genetic learning or memory and learning to adapt that behavior with reference to the immediate conditions of the environment and themselves. By trial and error the mother cat and the kittens can find that they can more consciously and directly effect satisfaction from the genetic drive to suckle and suck. I am sure the kittens learn how to be better suckers than their instincts tell them to be, because the satisfaction they derive from sucking acts as a motivation to improve it.

Let me give another example. Watching kittens is a fascinating pastime. Kittens seem to know how suckle, how to groom themselves, how to scratch, how to stretch and yawn, how to eat, how to eliminate, etc. None of these things do they do very well, nor do they excel in walking, climbing, and running. Sometimes I have watched a kitten in the midst of one action, say scratch, begin another action, say stand up, and have observed the apparent collision of two drives, to the bewilderment of the kitten. I hypothesize that there are general and not too sharply formed behaviors which are genetically originated which the kitten can see and experience. Being a kitten and having some measure of self-control and adaptability, he is able to consciously participate in this action so that it affords him the pleasure of the scratched itch where he is itching. He is doing two things then: using the genetic drive to scratch to his own immediate advantage and his learning to perfect his instinctive scratching is being reinforced due to the pleasure derived from that act.

When the kitten responds to the sound of the electric can opener and comes running, is it because he remembers that food usually follows that sound or is he only conditioned? Does he have the capacity to recall other times when that sound preceded food or is he living solely in the present and the same stimulus produces the same response because it has been reinforced by satisfaction? Can a cat or kitten consciously remember or is he merely a conditioned organism?

Our kittens learned very rapidly to use the kitty litter tray that the mother cat used. I believe that the mother cat served as a model for the kittens and they did as she did. When they do that as adult cats, do they remember seeing their mother doing that a long time ago? Or do they just live in the moment and continue what has been successful? How much can a cat consciously know about his being, about his environment? In that knowing which is so different from unconscious "knowing" he would have to be able to stand off from himself and see himself, a stance that we know humans can take. It is this self-consciousness, conscious recall, and capacity to take action other than genetic, conditioned, and modelled action that makes man peculiarly man among the other animals.

When a tree interacts with the elements, the record of the interaction is contained in the cell structure of the tree. For instance, if there has been a season of unusual wetness, the structure of the tree will demonstrate it. If the tree were situated in a place where there was constant strong wind from one direction, the structure of the tree would demonstrate it. In both cases the tree, if it survives, can be said to have learned how to respond to such conditions. The tree still lives entirely in the present and cannot "recall" that event except as it is itself an expression of that event.

When a kitten has its first encounters with humans and they have been satisfying or pleasant, its future encounters with humans will produce responses similar to the past ones but not necessarily because the cat remembers. The behavior of the cat is produced by his ongoing neurophysiological equipment which is present-oriented (to the best of our knowledge) and not past or future-oriented. He does not sit and contemplate humans and internally relish or fantasize how nice it is going to be to sit on their laps and be scratched and petted because he remembers how nice it was yesterday. (If he does, I apologize to all cats at once.)

Let us now consider the human. There is no doubt that he has the capacity for genetic recording or remembering. It can be demonstrated that he learns and remembers through conditioning. It can be said that he learns and remembers through mimicking. Man and perhaps some of the other higher animals seem to have an addition to the nervous system that permits a different kind of flexibility and adaptation denied the lesser beasts. I would like to postulate here that in life all those organisms that are equipped with sensing or recording mechanisms also have corollary mechanisms of action or response to that which they record. For instance, genetic recording is obviously hooked up to cellular structure and to instinctual behaviors, conditioning recording certainly produces behavior that replicates the original event, modeling recording certainly demonstrates the living capacity of some animals to do what they see being done. So with man's capacity to record events in other than genetic, conditioning, and modeling ways, and behavioral capacities to respond to such recording, we must add a behavioral capacity to respond to this new recording or learning mode. This behavioral mode is that of purposeful or controlled action and the recording mode that of monitoring all events on a replayable screen of consciousness. To elaborate, not only do humans have all that animals have in capacity to record the present on our very living cells and structures, but we have a new neurological consciousness, like an interior TV tape that we can play back and tinker with.

One of the results of this is that we as humans can sit back after a situation has been lived through and play back the event at our leisure and learn from it what we didn't have a chance to learn from it the first time. We as humans can learn while we are doing nothing but thinking. Writing a language and speaking a language seem to be reflections of the same process of recording events in retrievable and reusable packages in order to plot out the future with greater accuracy.

When I watch one of the kittens trying to find a way to return to the deck which he has learned to leap off of, I see his careful assessment (or so it seems) of distances, firmness of ground from which he is to take off, etc. All those preparations could be said to be anticipations of the future moment when he is to leap up to the beam, so he does plan for the future in some limited respects. But he cannot do any of that planning without being in contact with the ground he is about to leap from and having within sight the beam which he is trying to reach. We humans have a way to reconstruct interiorly through the symbols of words or some other devices as yet undiscovered in our minds, to consciously know and remember what it felt like to prepare to make that leap and even to reexperience some of the emotions of that event without the use of the conditioning effect of the ground or the beam. Perhaps it can be called conditoning but conditioning by the symbol of the external stimulus and not the physical reality of it. Symbols, then, can be experienced as real to humans and that is to their glory and to their pain.

Man's consciousness and the motor system connected to it provide the possibility for free will, if it indeed exists. Man's capacity for developing behavior patterns that are not connected to genetic memory includes the capacity to inhibit genetic behavior, for how could nongenetic behavior occur if instinctive behavior occurred willy-nilly when the individual had decided to take a more rational course of action? Sometimes our inhibition is not entirely successful for we can all recall situations when the unintended act was performed even after a rational course had been decided upon.

I would like now to return to the foetal structure which stimulated all this speculation on the meaning of memory. We can see now the many ways that man has at his disposal to learn, and to attain a repository of information. He is capable of genetic learning, conditioned learning, (trial and error learning is a type of conditioned learning), mimetic learning, and conscious recall or remembered learning. The aim of a psychomotor structure is to release the capacity of the human to recall, not only verbally, but, more important, in motor terms, all those events and interactions which have not resulted in satisfaction or pleasure or maturation, experiencing and "playing them out" again. This time the conscious, rational minds of the client and the therapist are available to glean new learnings, attitudes, conditionings, and modelings from the replaying, while permitting in a safe therapeutic environment the expression of energies and behaviors that had not been expressed in the original event, and adding to this memory positive relationships and experiences that had not been available in the original event.

Once again I ask the question: what is the point of going back? The problem is in the present and in how the future is to be dealt with. Obviously past learning controls the present and in a sense, predicts the future, that is, unless one gets a grasp on the patterns that have molded one's self and attempts to change them. There seem to be times when it is important for certain experiences to occur in the animal world, and if these experiences do not occur the negative results that accrue are irreversible. Simply removing the mother goat from infant goats for periods of an hour or more soon after birth and then returning the mother in a normal way thereafter can result in premature death for the kids. What is our adult client doing if only now he is seeking the nurture from his mother that he did not receive when he was an infant? How did he survive when the goat did not? Perhaps man can overcome certain environmental deficiencies by his capacity to experience symbols as real. Perhaps humans can derive nurture from other sources than the mother by using their capacity to inhibit and control their genetic life and replace that nurturance with symbols created in their own minds that somehow, albeit partially, overcome the deficit. Perhaps early as well as later he can confuse his inner symbolic life with concrete external life. How long does the human organism, waiting for the experiences it needs to grow with, remain receptive to new symbolic input through psychomotor structures? I believe it is possible, using the human power of recall, to reassemble those feeling states and emotions and ideas one had as an infant and place this experience, this new and partly symbolic and partly concrete experience, beside them as if the new experience had occurred in the past. He can, after that, experience the memory of his structure as if it had occurred in the actual past. When we watch a client in a structure are we only conditioning him to experience warmth from people now and in the future and not dealing with or affecting his past at all? If the past can not be reexperienced, how is it that the client can verbalize about feeling a different body size, experiencing a different body image, finding the quality of emotion that he identifies with being an infant, may even cry the way a baby cries, unexpectedly find a part of himself that doesn't know how to talk, that cannot move as an adult but only as a squirming helpless infant, that wishes to suckle, to clasp with his fingers, etc.?

When his body and his mind are in this state, are we to interrupt him and say, "Listen, you are an adult; stop acting like a baby. You cannot go back. You will have to face the fact that you were deprived as an infant and understand that those feelings have nothing to do with you now." All these things said would be true but would we be helping him to truly face the present or the future?

What we do do is to create a structure and accommodation where all his needs can be met, not by us literally in the group with him, but by us symbolically as the parents he never had and which he deserved to have. We attempt to achieve the fullest match between his needs and our responses, and inevitably the client achieves a level of satisfaction and relaxation that is far distant from the agitation he showed earlier. He can also be afforded the negative parents toward whom an enormous amount of rage would be forthcoming, permitting his experience with the positive parents to remain unambiguous and undisturbed. When he is through the structure and reexperiences his present sense of himself, he may have a new picture of the world on which to base his future expectations. He is now in a position to anticipate that there might indeed be people who can understand him and relate satisfyingly to him, and he can begin to grow from there.

How is it that the client can recall and reproduce so graphically at that time the emotions and actions of an infant? Perhaps
it is that humans remember those things that did not turn out
well and forget those things that did. For instance, we are more
likely to recall those questions in an exam that we could not
answer properly than those which were a snap. When things
do not turn out well we experience frustration. When we experience frustration we get angry. If we find ways to express the
frustration and anger, we have still to overcome the frustrating
experience. If perhaps we find no way to overcome the frustrating experience and no way to express the frustration and rage,
we are in a bad place. Humans seem to have the capacity to
inhibit, as described earlier, genetic and other types of memory
and learning and also the capacity to recall. We think that in
psychomotor therapy we are taking advantage of that recalling
capacity in permitting inhibited and possibly misdirected energies more direct motor expression, which then permits more
rational choices. It is hypothesized that unless they are so expressed the misdirected emotional energies distort and contra-
vene the rational energies.

If we were to take an adult cat that had not been well treated
in its infancy and place it with a group of other cats, would
it regress to kittenhood and try to suckle and get angry and
bite in memory of the absent nipple of the mother cat? We
know that it would not. Our cat would be locked into the "now
of itself." It could not recall as our human client could. It could
not overcome the vicissitudes of its inferior infancy. It would
have to bear the results of its history, whatever they were. I
do not think that it would be sufficient for our client to change
if he only understood what had happened to him when he
was young. What would make him truly believe that the future
could or would be better? If nothing beyond that, a positive-
ending structure might make him inclined to believe that at
least those in his group could be nice to him, but I believe
it does that and a good deal more.

Animals certainly must have a screen of consciousness which is somehow recorded interiorly and mentally. Animals remember which is their territory and which is another animal's. Perhaps there are markers—visual, auditory and olfactory—which assist them in this recall each time they move through the territory, but they do remember pathways and locales they have been through before. The question is, how much innate capacity have they for internal representation of a symbolic form? Bees are known to have the capacity to report the location of pollen sources to other bees. Isn't this working with symbols and then manipulating the symbols for the purposes of the future? However, has the bee decided to do this or is he locked into his instinctive equipment which has the limited capacity to symbolize only events having to do with pollen gathering? Perhaps the appropriate attitude should be that animals and insects show rudimentary forms of symbol making and symbol use whereas man has a very large capacity for the same.

Dreaming

Animals dream. I have often seen my German shepherd in what appeared to be similar to a human dream state. He will move in a way that is reminiscent of running, his breathing becomes rapid and he utters small barks. Is his motor system simply turning over in his sleep without a concomitant representation in his head of some encounter that would include running and barking? My inclination is to believe that he is dreaming, meaning that he must have some capacity to symbolize events and then recall them as if real, at least in a dream state. If that is the case, then dogs and other animals that dream have that inner, "playbackable" symbolic screen that only humans are supposed to have. There must then be two different orders of screen, that of dreaming which is an automatic or not consciously directed process, and that of thinking and planning which is of a conscious and future-directed process. I would like to hypothesize that dreaming is a somewhat "bodiless" state where the inner symbolic representations of reality are manipulated by automatic processes in the brain for mastery of internal energies and external events. By using the term *somewhat bodiless* I mean to point out that emotional events in the animal world are usually responded to behaviorally but that in a dream those neural impulses and glandular discharges can be shunted to another arena which is essentially bodiless but which has some small measure of motoric discharges (as the grunts and squirmings we have all experienced and seen in others will attest) and sensory input, as rapid eye movement studies show, for the eyes seem to be following the movement "seen" in the dream. Is the dream state the early neurological model for symbol formation and manipulation that we see in conscious thinking? The sequence toward the evolution of symbolic thought processes could be first a sensory-motor experience, then the symbolic representation, or automatic memory of that in a dream which includes some sensory-motor content, and then the conscious manipulation of those symbols without (or with negligible) sensory-motor experience.

What I am seeking to describe is that mental and behavioral capacity that man has for dealing with the inner and outer world on three levels: that of experiential interaction with concrete reality, that of dreaming, and that of symbolic thinking. I believe that included in what we call mental illness can be the misapplication of energies that would go toward interaction with concrete reality and expending them on those processes that are merely the inner screens for the symbolic experience and manipulation of that concrete reality. Said more simply, mental illness can include the confusion or fusion of those three arenas, with the patient attempting to relate or interact to his own inner processes as if they were external reality. What we attempt to do with mental patients in psychomotor therapy structures is to take that interactive energy and direct it toward other people (accommodators) and wean it away from its application to one's own symbol-making processes.

This could explain the physical appearance and behavior of certain mental patients who are described as having motor difficulties. That energy that would mobilize their bodies to respond in a concrete, interactive, instinctive way with the environment could be used in a "bodiless" symbolic way described in the dream and thought state. *Schizoid* in this description would mean split away from the body and its normal interactions with other bodies. And the "concrete" thinking of those patients could be explained as treating and experiencing the symbols of thought and dream states as if they were indeed the concrete reality they are confusing it with. The equation seems to include the possibility of a simple reversal. Inner symbol processes are experienced as concrete interactions and concrete interactions are experienced as inner thought or symbol processes.

Life seems to move toward an ever greater and more conscious control of the environment. Our genes carry information regarding successful control of and adaptation to the environment, and the process of natural selection is the means which nature uses to test new modes of control and interaction. By what seems to be a random manipulation of the microscopic shapes of genes, adaptation of behavior to the macroscopic environment can be improved. Of course most of the random manipulations result in monsters and failures; however, those fortuitous combinations that result in a greater control over the environment replicate themselves and are passed down as valuable or at the least nondestructive information for the species.

Another stage for the testing of new information that would be valuable to the species and to the individual is dreaming where microscopic, possibly random, symbol manipulations could demonstrate new possibilities in the macroscopic world of real events. Dreams could offer two uses to humans. One, the commonly accepted one where those emotions that cannot be expressed during the day in reality can be expressed in the "bodiless" dream state, and two, the learning of new behavior and response possibilities from the random manipulation of the symbols of daily events. Certainly we see enough monsters as natural selection and mutation must create monsters in our dreams, but a certain percentage of the manipulations would perhaps prove valuable and lead toward new adaptations and better control over the environment. Probably both those processes go on simultaneously, explaining both the familiarity and the originality of dreams.

The most recent stage for the testing of new information is the stage of conscious thought. There the manipulations of the microscopic symbols of reality are more conscious and more directed, thereby providing the more rapid explosion of new information and new controls we as humans are now experiencing. When humans first became humans, this process must have been relatively slow since the external symbols, the written words, did not appear until fairly recently. With the advent of a system which permitted the transmission of this new knowledge from person to person in a concrete form, a repository, much like the microscopic repository within the genes, is assembled which is used to salvage the individual knowledge for the group and for future generations. With the advent of instantaneous communication media, the dissemination of this new information is now becoming global which should result in a relatively global culture.

In short, the slow moving evolutionary process of random manipulation of information is being accelerated through the use of dreams and conscious thought, placing in man's hands the possibility of conscious evolution of the species. Should man's dreams and man's thoughts be contaminated, so to speak, with confused application of interactive energy, or in other words, should this rapid evolution and control of the world be infected with the mental illness of misdirected psychic energies, the result could be disastrous. This, then, is a plea for the rational use of thought and technology toward the goal of species and life improvement and not species and life destruction.

Now with this hypothesis regarding the evolution of dreams and thought and symbol-making processes, we see a greater differentiation between man and the other animals. We have also highlighted another aspect in the use of psychomotor structures. A structure might be seen as an invented arena that taps the human potential to learn from the manipulation of dream materials and conscious thought materials using sensory-motor memory and reinforcement, as well as instinctive, interactional modes of relationship. It also uses some of the qualities of "playing," whereby certain roles can be tested and experienced. In sum, psychomotor structures offer an extremely wide range of learning, growth, and clarification opportunities other than the mere acting out of bodily impulses. I will go into exhaustive detail further on in this book, describing many structures so that the kinds of controls, limits, and freedoms that are permitted in a structure will be entirely clear to the reader. But first, in the next chapter, I would like to return to the question "What does the young human organism need?"

CHAPTER 3

We left our newly conceived infant organism in the process of—what is the appropriate word?—planting in, relating, joining, fusing, attaching, embedding, becoming part of, sticking to, touching, feeling, sensing, . . . loving, being loved by, the uterine wall. I raise the possibilities within all those words because what goes on between what is to become child and what is part of mother is so fundamental to all levels of sensing, relating, loving, being, etc., that will go on or not go on in the future. If there is to be love between humans, it must have its primitive beginnings here. If there is to be relating between two humans it must be rooted here. On the negative side, if there is to be difficulty in individuating the personality—that is, in becoming a separate, discrete, identifiable, autonomous, single individual—it must begin with the difficulties created by the necessity for the parent organism to be so materially and concretely a part of the child organism in order to provide the child organism with capacity to survive and develop. The success of the individuating process depends on the quality and type of interactions between parent and child during pregnancy and the quality and type of interactions after birth and during early childhood.

To be separate and to know that one is separate is the task and fate of the human individual. Animals, in the natural course of events, seem to be able to become individuals relatively easily. However, in their individuality they are without the tensions, apparently, of fully knowing the implications and responsibilities of their separateness. In another sense they have not become individuals because they are fully embedded in their instincts, and it is to their instincts that the credit for the individuality must go. In the animal world the individuating process is mainly physiological. Certain physiological processes must be carried out in a certain order for the animal to survive infancy and become adult. The same is true for the human infant, but built upon the base of those physiological processes must be certain psychological or relationship or attitudinal processes.

Let me clarify the two issues that are beginning to surface in this discussion. The first is the development of the individual out of the universal with the paradoxical addition of the necessity for the individual to recognize both the individual and universal aspects of his being and to achieve a balanced relationship between the two. The second is the relationship and differences between physiological and psychological events. Both these issues must be understood and dealt with in order to understand the implications of the rearing process in human life. It is incumbent on the parent to make the proper decisions regarding these issues in the development of the child. If the proper decisions are not made, it is incumbent on future teachers and/or therapists to make up for the lacks in the upbringing and to provide what has been missing.

It must be said here that among other things, this book represents the philosophical, therapeutic, and educational viewpoints that I have arrived at from doing my work. My understanding can come only from my own experience as a human being, parent, teacher, and therapist living in this particular culture at this particular time, watching hundreds of people from this culture in thousands of hours of structure time while considering myself a member of the world community and wondering what is best from all those standpoints. It must be understood then, that all my statements regarding universality, individuality, the best possible conditions for human growth, etc., are to be seen in the light of my particular culture. While it is my hope to transcend or see beyond my own provincial guidelines, one is ever a child of one's own time. Yet I extend these distillations of my experience in the hope that they may fall on fertile or accepting ground, there to provide the receiver with some value in the way of a more satisfying life.

It seems to me that it is important for a child to find those factors in his personality that lead him to a relationship with others, nature, and the unknown without feeling that they are foreign to him or indeed that they could be of a different material universe than his. For he is made of the same basic particles that all nature is made of and must share in some of the same history with all living things. At the same time he is the only one living in his own skin during his time of life and place of life, and no one can see, experience, and relate to the world in precisely the way he sees, experiences, and relates to the world. He also must do those things which are important to the world at large, in an ecological sense, without doing injury to his own individual needs and vice versa.

There is an analogy in the relationships between universal and individual, and physiological and psychological, in that individuality is abstracted from or rises from universality and that which is psychological is abstracted or arises from what is physiological. (Clearly a human being must be able to deal with problems of individuality, psychology, and abstractions for animals apparently cannot.)

Man's first experience with relating is a profound joining. The sperm and egg relate to each other by joining. The fertilized egg relates to the wall of the uterus by joining it physiologically. This second joining however is only a temporary one in the physiological sense. In the psychological sense the joining is more correctly understood as relating. I want to point out that all relating has its history and roots in having been joined, all that is psychological has its history or roots in the physiological, all abstractions have their roots in the concrete, all that is individual has its roots in the universal.

As the fertilized egg could not live without joining the wall of the uterus, and by extension, the mother, a human being cannot live without relating to other human beings. This is more true in the earlier years, for man can, in later years, having accumulated a history of real relationships, live on the memories of those years while in actuality being relatively or entirely isolated. That is, having had sufficient quantities of actual experience with people, he can, albeit with difficulty, if he must, relate to the symbolic abstractions of those experiences—his memories—and still remain a human being. Whereas a child who has been abandoned, and in one of those rare circumstances been reared by animals or is old enough to forage for food himself in isolation from other humans, will likely be permanently distorted and unlike most human beings, that is, if he lives at all. What I am suggesting here is that we can as humans relate to symbols as if they were real and with some success, so long as they have been well rooted in concrete reality, but should that symbol-relating propensity occur too soon, before sufficient concrete experiences have been assimilated, distortions of the psyche are the result. We have to be able to live in the concrete world and in the abstract, symbolic world, but the timing and the balance between the two worlds is of utmost importance in the rearing situation. The same is true of the balance between individuality and universality. The parent must assist in the process of teaching the child that his needs and feelings are important and of value, while also giving him the opportunity to learn that his relationship of giving and caring for others beyond himself is to be developed for the satisfaction of others and for the satisfaction of that aspect of himself that needs and is capable of enjoying the role of giving.

What does the uterus give to the fertilized egg? Everything that it needs from the outside world at that time. The egg has genetic information that uses the nurturant flow from the placenta to grow on. The foetus is supported and carried by the uterus and is then free of the need to counter the force of gravity. The walls of the uterus protect the growing foetus, with the assistance of the cushioning effect of the amniotic fluid. The walls of the uterus represent flexible but limiting barriers to its growth and powers. As the foetus stretches and moves in the uterus it comes in contact with the limitations imposed by the size of the womb and "learns" that there are some things it cannot do.

We who are doing psychomotor therapy have become accustomed to listing the functions of the uterus as: nurturance, support, protection, and limits. These four concrete relationships with the foetus imply a fifth, abstract relationship—that of respect. It could be metaphorically said that the uterus respects the foetus in that it responds to it by supplying those things necessary for its survival. I do not mean to personalize the uterus by using the term "respect" but to lead up to the idea that the four basic functions of the uterus are similar to the manner of relating that the mother (and then later the father) has with the child after it is born. The mother correctly could be said to view the child with respect when she ministers to the child's needs for nurturance, support, protection, and limits. The child who has become an adult, autonomous person, who has learned to nurture, support, protect, and limit himself can be said to have self-respect. Thus there can be seen to be three levels or stages which must be passed through and which deal with the same phenomena, rising from the concrete and physiological to the abstract and psychological. All those moves and relationships must be carried out in such a way as to provide maximum matching with the needs of the growing organism-person without subverting his future needs and capacity to carry out those matchings and needs for himself. Parenthetically, I must include the fact that the adult client must be able to redo or reexperience this trip from the concrete to the abstract without losing the capacity to experience in the concrete and physiological realm. His growth should not leave him in the dubious position of being able *only* to live and experience on the symbolic and abstract levels. Living calls for the widest possible ranges of interactions and feelings and demands a balance of all human capacities.

The first level is the intrauterine level which is physiological, concrete, real, cellular, unconscious, automatic. The analogy with the tree would be most appropriate here—the seed being the fertilized egg, the placenta wall being the earth, the growing tree being the growing foetus. Comparatively speaking, the greatest learning and growth of the foetus at the earliest points is cellular and not behavioral; although there is movement of the foetus quite early, it is a mere suggestion of what is to come.

The second level is the postnatal level which is interactive and movement-oriented. It is still the realm of the real, but is already in transition toward the abstract. It is the time of organ use and further differentiation and motor use and differentiation. It is a time of consciousness for the mother and growing consciousness for the child. A second stage in this level includes the interaction with the father and the entrance into the world beyond the protective home.

The third level is the relationship with the world at large including conscious peer, autonomous, individual, symbolic aspects. It deals with finding a place and a role in the larger society through one's own efforts and capacities. Obviously, success at this level is dependent on success at earlier levels.

Ordinarily, very little goes wrong in the first intrauterine level; however I have seen some clients whose responses, actions, and reactions in a structure lead me to wonder about the varying kinds of environments that mothers provide because of their physical structure or psychological attitudes toward the growing foetus. I wonder if some foetuses are uncomfortable due to the restrictive structure of the mother's body; to the unpleasant character of the mother's movements; to actual blows felt by the infant caused by falls of the mother or blows administered to the mother by others; to the unpleasant quality of the mother's voice; to the strongly varying heartbeat of the mother; and to a possibly unpleasant chemistry of the amniotic fluid.

Autism Versus Autonomy

The goal of the growing organism-person is to become an autonomous individual. In order for this to happen, the person has to have sufficient concrete experiences with the mother and the father which then can be internalized or internally symbolized and available to the person as information or learning which he can apply for himself autonomously. There must be a stage of dependent concrete relationships before autonomy can occur and independence from others result. If, during the stage when the person should be dependent, the intrauterine environment or the home environment fails to provide the necessary concrete experiences, the child-organism has the humanly possible alternative of providing for itself what was missing. This too-soon turning toward one's self for one's basic needs can be understood as an autistic rather than autonomous solution to survival. When this autistic solution occurs, one's interactive energies which are other-oriented, become oriented toward portions of the self and the individual turns away from relating to the external world, just at those times when he most needs the external world to develop normally.

One possibility, in the absence of concrete, behavioral interactions with the mother, is for the child to relate to certain symbols, within himself or in the inanimate world, in lieu of the concrete objects he is missing. Then, instead of learning to manipulate and control the external world to provide his needs, he turns to learning to control his internal world, confusing it symbolically with the external world, and becomes within himself the individual *and* the world, without learning to make the trip from universal to individual but remaining fused with the universal.

It has often been noted that autistic children have high intellectual capacities. Perhaps, by an accident of genetic structure, the symbol-making capacities of those children have been too rapidly developed, and those capacities too soon attract the interest and interactive energy of the child away from the less manipulable real world.

Some Responses to Failures in the Satisfaction of the Four Basic Needs

If there has been a failure of the mother in the realm of nurture, the child is forced to postpone the development that should accrue from the oral and tactile input and to seek alternate figures and means to satisfy needs. Since the flow of milk to the mouth is second, only, in importance to the infant, to the flow of blood through the umbilical cord in establishing an interactive, learning, growing relationship with the world for the future, a failure of the mother in the nurturant role has disastrous consequences. Of course there must be sufficient milk of one kind or another to keep the child alive physiologically, but milk is not enough. There must be sufficient opportunities for sucking for its own sake and sufficient touching and cuddling for its own sake. In the absence of those neural inputs around the mouth and the surface of the body in general, other types of neural inputs seem to be able to be substituted. Once these substitute inputs have become integrated into the child's life processes, they acquire the same value for survival as the normal process of suckling and cuddling and are very difficult to change. They contribute to the style of interaction that the child maintains throughout the rest of its life unless there is an intercession by way of therapy or intense educational processes.

The input must be experienced and because of the flexible nature of man's psychic being, because of man's capacity to treat symbols as real, and because of man's capacity to treat his own body and his own movements symbolically (there is symbolic action as well as symbolic words in man's inner being), he can take in cooing sounds or music in his ear with the same affection that he takes in milk and cuddling and impute to them the same importance. In a sense then, the ear can be interchanged with the mouth as the organ for nurturant input; the ear becomes symbolically confused with the mouth, so to speak.

Primary process in this instance becomes not only a primitive flow from the individual back into the universal in the sense of all organs being interchangeable to the unconscious, but an expression of the higher capacities of man to symbolize, again not only to use thought symbolically but to use body and action symbolically.

To return to nurturance distortions, the ear-mouth confusion is relatively benign. Consider the confusions that can occur if the mother is unduly concerned with the anus of the child. We have seen instances where the client has been given enemas regularly from the first week of life on through most of childhood. If the father rather than the mother is the one who tends to offer nurturance by way of bottle feeding and cuddling, there may be repercussions in that the organ of giving may become confused and may even shift from the mother's breast to the father's penis. This shift has shown up in therapy quite often.

Negative Nurturance

Sometimes a child is not fed and cuddled at all in its infancy but is regularly abused physically and rejected. Significantly, this type of neural input is precisely what the child learns to live with. The child learns to "eat" or be nurtured by pain and rejection. This child, when he is grown, might unwittingly place himself in situations where he is physically abused and rejected, all the while unhappy and miserable that that is his fate (and not seeing that this is precisely the type of interaction he seeks). This we label negative nurturance.

Primary Mode of Relationship

We have learned in psychomotor therapy to be on the look-out for those modes of relationship which can be understood to be replicas of the distortions in the nurturant cuddling phase and which the client tends to reproduce in the therapeutic sessions. We have learned to watch what it is that the client demands in the way of treatment from the therapist and from other group members, speculating that he will then "eat" or consume the response that he has generated. Some patients place themselves in a situation where they will be humiliated and degraded symbolically, made to "eat shit." Some clients tend to make the group or the therapist want to strike them and hit them, figuratively trying to "eat fist." Some clients try to provoke a powerful sexual reaction in all those whom they come in contact with, including the therapist and group members, and this can be seen as an attempt to arouse sexual feelings in order to "receive or eat cock."

One of the goals in therapy is to bring out these confusions and to clarify them by giving the appropriate organs the appropriate input. It is hypothesized that those styles of interaction that are compulsive and unsatisfying might have their roots in insufficient and unsatisfying nurturant experiences. We attempt to provide the client with the fulfillment of the oral and tactile needs he has missed. However, it is not possible simply to tell the client to lie down on an accommodator's lap and pretend to suckle at her breast, while in actuality sucking on a fleshy portion of her hand or arm. It is first necessary to permit the client to move entirely as his own body wishes at the moment of his structure and to keep in mind the problem and clarify it when the situation permits. An important point to note is that in order to return successfully to the mouth as the organ of nurturant input, one must first gather the interactive energy that is being applied to other organs or the sucking that one does will be forced and meaningless. We will go into detail regarding this when discussing individual structures.

Support Needs

Just as the foetus needs the support of the womb to give it mobility, the infant, after birth, needs the supporting arms and bodies of the parents to carry him about until such time as he can walk and carry himself about. The child needs the guiding presence of the parent when he begins to walk so that, should he trip, he can grasp for the hand of the nearby parent for stability and support. It is important that a good balance between dependence and independence be established by the parent so that the child's natural curiosity and mobility are not overcome by a too solicitous parent. The child has to get a sense of the parents' "being there" when he needs them. This shows up later on the psychological level in the parents' backing up the child in events in which the child needs moral support. The child must have the sense of the parent's being behind him when he attempts to deal with a challenging situation. Quite often in a structure, when support issues are arising, the client may feel wobbly in the knees and wish to be held or carried, feeling unable to carry himself and needing the strength and support of parent figures.

Sometimes when a client in a support issue is offered the ministrations of strong parents, the client reports that he feels his own knees stiffening at the approach of the parents. He may comment that he doesn't feel he can depend on his parents and that he would rather depend on himself. When questioned about his past the client may relate that he was the eldest in the family and had to take on the responsibilities of the family support as the father was ill, etc. He may recall that in crises when he needed his parents they were never there, etc. Once again we are faced with a situation in which the client, not having received the quality of experience he needs from his parents, develops too soon (and with relationship-damaging consequences) the capacity to make do for himself out of his young resources. Of course it is important for children to learn to stand on their own feet but the timing is of the essence.

Too soon and the child may be unable ever to receive from other people even when it is reasonable to do so, too late and the child may become overdependent and unable to care for himself. The physical areas of the body that seem to be involved in the support experience are under the knees and thighs, and on the back.

Protection Needs

The walls of the uterus protect the child from the force of overpowering interactive events. They shield the child from the potentially hostile elements in the environment. Symbolically and literally the arms and bodies of the parents carry on the protection after the child is born. The parent's function is to stave off hostile attacks, literally blows, from the child. Symbolically the parent holds off the threatening energies from the environment. The parent keeps at arms length those events and relationships that would overwhelm the inner coherence of the child (remember the rock being hit by another rock?).

If the child is not sufficiently protected from hostile energies, he can either develop his own strength too soon and learn to combat external threat by becoming "hard" and not permitting anything to "get to him." Or he can succumb to the excessive energies that come his fragile way and he can be overwhelmed, invaded and destroyed by the forces that are greater than the force of his personal coherence. In the absence of adequate physical strength, the child may find symbolic inner processes or thoughts which can give him supernatural power to drain his interactive energy from external targets and intensify his relationship to his own inner processes.

Experience indicates that the bodily expression of the parent's mode of protection is in the circular embrace of the arms. Sometimes a client who is in need of this protection while in a structure will wrap his own arms around himself and when offered strong parental figures will ask them to hold him tightly. The two parents can make a circle of their arms around the client, making a shield with their arms and bodies, and they can verbalize how they will protect the client from real or imagined threatening forces. (Of course it is important to ascertain whether the client is experiencing the threat from within, as of his own feelings. That is responded to differently, but that will be dealt with later.) In the issue of protection the father seems more emphasized than the mother, as the client seems to search for and find the strength of the father as indicative of protection. When the client is being held, he may wish to be held very tightly, to hold on to the arms of his good parents, and to seek physical and verbal reassurance that they are strong enough to take care of him.

"Promise Me You'll Always Be There"

Frequently, in a structure a client will beseech the parents to vow that they will always care for him and always be there when he needs them. Although this plea on the surface might appear as a negative indication of one's ability or willingness to become independent and autonomous it seems to me more definitely a necessary and important aspect of the parental relationship with the child—the parent must satisfy the child's needs for constancy and stability. By answering "yes" to the child's wish, we are not undermining the child's drive toward self-reliance; we are giving him a psychological and symbolic sense of firmness, constancy and stability. If one's parents have been that constant, while at the same time offering the child ample opportunities for practicing self-reliance, the results will certainly be in favor of independence and the discovery of those firm, stable qualities in one's self.

The Need to Be Limited

In order to be an individual, one needs to have a shape. In order to have a shape, there must be a boundary or a limit delineating the individual. A child has no sense of his power until he tests it in a concrete, behavioral way. He must live in an atmosphere where it is permissible for him to exercise all the genetic energies at his disposal, from love to hate, without fear that his energies will overcome either him or his world. He must learn that he is master of his genetic being and that he is not "a bump on his omnipotent emotions." Some clients have expressed the fear that should they let their feelings go, they would be washed away as so many sand buildings under the force of the tide and waves on the seashore. In a structure the good parents let the child client know that they are strong enough to "handle" him—that they can take all his emotions without being overwhelmed, destroyed, killed, or raped. The emotion of hate which is being experienced as an overwhelming, world-destroying force can be tested and limited in a structure, not by accommodating it as would be done with ordinary levels of anger but by literally containing it. The entire group participates in this, acting as extensions of the good parents. The client lies on the floor (which should be well carpeted) or a mat or mattress and the group members place their hands on his legs, torso, and arms. The good parents usually place themselves at opposite sides of the client's head so that he will be most conscious of them and be able to hear what they may say. Then the client can attempt to "kill" the group, the world, the parents or whomever, attempting to get free while doing so. The amount of energy that this permits is impressive. Some male clients may need seven or more people to hold them down. They may scream, shriek, froth, and rage, but the group and the good parents hold them down while letting them know that they are not afraid of their emotions and that they can keep the clients from killing them.

It is interesting how often the client will describe his reaction to this restraint with relief and pleasure. He may comment that he tried with every ounce of his strength and was sure that he would throw everyone off and go beserk but found that he could not do it and was surprised to find that he liked that and that he could relax a good deal more after the effort.

This exercise is reminiscent of the nonverbal exercise of breaking in or breaking out, used in some encounter groups; however, in this case if the client were permitted to break out it would reinforce his omnipotent fantasies and fears, precisely what we are trying to contain!

An important factor to observe is whether the client is ready for such a limiting structure. One, it might be that he is not *at the moment* experiencing the intense feelings which he is fearful will overwhelm him. Having him go through this structure half-heartedly will serve no good effect. Two, by pointed questioning the group leader must ascertain whether the client is experiencing the constraint as a rape or invasion of himself. If that is what appears to be happening, the therapist should terminate the holding at once, to avoid reinforcing a potential negative nurturance where the client seeks to be overcome by the group.

A parent or parents who give the message to their child that he is too much for them to handle is playing into the hands of the child's fantasies of omnipotence. Of course a child should not be overly limited or he will feel trapped and constrained where his emotional energies are concerned. Being limiting in a punitive way would tend to result in an invasion of the child by the very figures who were supposed to protect him from invasion. That is why the good father figure in a structure will often say that he uses his strength to protect the child and not to invade the child. The bodily symbolic and concrete posture for this is to have the father figure facing the outside world with his arms extended in a protective fashion with his back to the client, demonstrating that the power of his hands and arms is directed towards the world and not towards him.

If in reality a child is not sufficiently limited he may respond in a variety of ways. He may abuse those around him in a thoughtless way; he may be fearful of his emotions and repress them following an event in which he may have caused serious or even near fatal injury; he may fantasize that his untouched and untested emotions are all powerful and not use these energies for any real situation.

There seems to be a connection between limiting and guilt (superego processes if you will). Consider the following event: During a structure with a student group of clinical psychology graduate students, the limiting was attempted with the student in a standing position. Even though there were a large number of people in the group, including a majority of males, the student almost broke free when the group members who were holding his legs lost their grasp of him. He was successfully contained however and when the structure was over the student verbalized his reaction to the moment when it seemed he could break free. He said that he fantasized that if he broke free he would plunge for the large windows and crash through them (we were on the fifteenth floor of the building). My interpretation of this event is that the student, unable to be limited by the parent figures (who are really to be understood as external symbols of his own ego), handled the force of his hostility by turning it toward himself. My hypothesis is that when ego controls break down, sometimes superego controls deflect the energy away from the environment and toward the self. Guilt and punishment seem to me to be part of the process by which the individual places the needs of the rest of the world alongside the needs of himself. The superego can be seen as an expression of an individual's awareness of his universal components in a nonomnipotent way.

CHAPTER 4

The ideal relationship of the child with the parents is not a static but an active and changing one. The process of becoming an autonomous, competent human being with a sense of one's own identity and place in the world is a resultant of a complex interaction of energies, behaviors, relationships, attitudes, and genetic processes. There is a multilevel, simultaneous, mutually interdependent nexus of forces which is the center of the experience of being human itself. There are some elements of this process which I have not described in psychomotor terms, which task I would like to undertake now.

Interactive Energy

Life is essentially interactive. By that I mean what is implied in those words beginning Chapter 1, "Life comes from life. Life needs and relates to life." Experience in psychomotor therapy leads me to believe that the primary equation in life is feeling (or sensing) leading to action, leading to interaction. Life seeks targets for its own expression and growth. The concept of interactive energy includes five distinctive arenas, each with its own sensory-motor apparatus and type of target (an expansion of the three motor systems described in my book *Movement in Psychotherapy*). I call these five systems reflexive body righting, metabolic-vegetative, interpersonal, material (impersonal), and verbal-symbolic. When working with the interactive-energy concept in the interpersonal arena, I use a diagram of three concentric circles representing three spheres. The inner circle is the source of the interactive energy, the head or the brain. The next circle represents the body or action sphere. The outer circle represents the "other body" or interaction sphere.

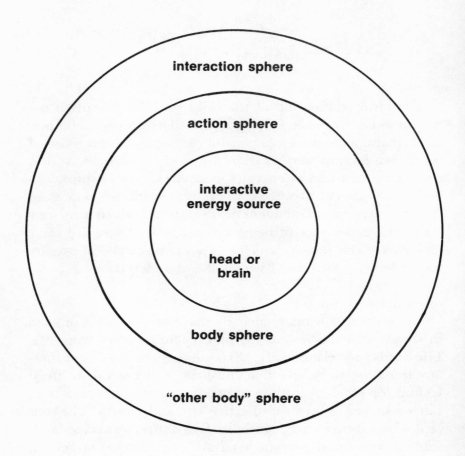

Experience in psychomotor therapy has led me to believe
that there are archetypical pathways for the expression of interactive energy which result in archetypical patterns of behavior.
Just as the behavior of the fertilized egg demonstrates that the
egg "knows" how and where to attach to the uterine wall, it
shows also that it "knows" how to receive the "responses" of
the uterine wall. The primitive, archetypical behavior of the
infant demonstrates that he "knows" how to respond to the
ministrations of the mother. I am suggesting that on some prim-

itive archetypical level, *action* itself "knows" its own effects and responses. It is as if the shapes of action which the body makes are in a jigsaw-puzzle-like match with aspects of the environment. For example, when a person expresses anger, he may swing his fist. The shape of this action anticipates the reaction of someone being struck and falling back. Implied here is that all parts of nature are connected and that the parts "know" each other. Life is not lived in a vacuum. All life is interrelated.

Consider the molecular structure of chemical interactions. When two elements combine to form a compound, they do not simply "hang around" each other in some loose fashion but their molecular faceting engages in a concrete, almost mechanical fashion. In an analogous sense, the matching facetings "know" each other; and through their "knowing" they are relating, sharing, and changing in a growing "learningful" way. Recent research in enzyme action suggests that the enzyme functions by having surfaces which geometrically match the surfaces of the elements of the two molecules which they will unite or separate. (Perhaps the analogy of the catalyst is appropriate for the educator, therapist. He should have "surfaces" that match the student, client, and the material). It seems possible to me that even at our advanced level of evolution and complexity, we contain some vestiges of this primitive way of relating. It also seems possible to me that when we are at our most primitive levels, in our infancy for instance, we are most likely to show archetypical and stereotypic actions and responses.

In psychomotor structures, I have learned to watch the body of the client to see where on his body the interactive energy can be perceived and then to attempt to arrange the accommodation by means of the "other bodies" of the group members to "match" the potential behavior that is appearing. An adult client is not a primitive infant and what can be seen on his body is a complex, symbolic conglomerate of tensions and imminent behaviors and inhibitions. How is this sorted out? First let us return to the infant. The infant is still pretty well locked into his instincts and primitive stereotypic reflexes. His interactions with his mother are fairly concrete, particularly where his nursing, tactile, and support needs are concerned. His mouth comes in contact with the nipple and breast of the mother and his little body is supported and cuddled in his mother's arms. His head and trunk are the particular areas experiencing the support, and his mouth and general skin surfaces the areas experiencing the nurturance and cuddling. In psychomotor terms his mouth is energized and "wants" to come into active contact sucking on the breast of the mother. An adult in a structure might not only experience a reawakening of the sucking mode but feel the clasping and squeezing in his hands, as well as the curling and uncurling of the toes, that are evinced by nursing infants. The baby's curled body position may indicate the shape the mother's arms and torso should make to match it in "counter-response."

The clasping and unclasping hands of the infant seem to "want" to squeeze the breast of the mother, as nursing kittens press their paws against the breast of the mother cat. The curling and uncurling toes do not seem to show specific goal orientation. It is possible, however, that the toes are an expression of pleasurable feeling without having an object. It is also possible that the feet are behaving in some tandem fashion with the clasping and unclasping of the hands and represent a kind of neural "echo" of the hands.

What have we been saying? We are saying that humans rapidly go from the stage of simple, mechanical, direct, concrete, interactions with the world to complex, symbolic, indirect, abstract interactions with the world. These abstractions should be based on satisfying concrete experiences and that is the type of ordering that we try to achieve in psychomotor structures. Since the human psyche is so flexible, and since the human propensity for symbolizing body parts and actions and the body parts and actions of target figures is rapid, there is great opportunity for fusion and confusion of basic actions and interactions. We see the work cut out for us in structures to include the tasks of finding the place where the interactive energy is appearing, finding the target and the part of the body aimed for in the target, and then attempting to make an ordered and clarifying reconstruction of what would be most appropriate, satisfying, and unfused. The difficulty is compounded by the fact that human emotions and feelings can be very plastic and also used symbolically. The task then, is threefold: (1) to assist in the unfusing and clarification of the confusion of the emotions (energy sphere); (2) to assist in the unfusing and clarification of the organs or body parts involved in the expression (body sphere); (3) to assist in the unfusing and clarification of the confusion of target figures (other body sphere).

Interactive Energy Directed toward Symbolic Alternatives

The goal of the interactive-energy schema is related to the goal of the concepts-regarding-infant-needs schema with the addition of the symbol-making process. Let me see if I can tie them together. It is understood that a foetus and then an infant needs certain types of interaction which include nurturance, support, etc., and that if those needs are not met by the parents he will find alternatives to those needs. Those alternatives include his own body processes, and both these processes and his own thoughts treated symbolically. It can be seen then that the symbol-making capacity of the human can be used as an auxiliary system of controlling the needed input from the environment. Using symbols that way is not the highest use to which symbol making can be put, but it is a survival technique which permits much adaptation to inferior life circumstances. It promotes survival but hinders future growth due to the stultifying nature of the fusions and confusions that result. Thus when fusions and confusions show up in a structure, an attempt is made not only to clarify them but to provide the client with the direct satisfaction of his basic child needs with relation to the appropriate figure. However, therapeutic intervention must include the use of the energy that has been bound up with the inappropriate symbolic actions and targets. This is demonstrated in the following diagram, dotted lines indicating what should have occurred and would have been more satisfying and the solid lines what actually did provide satisfactions.

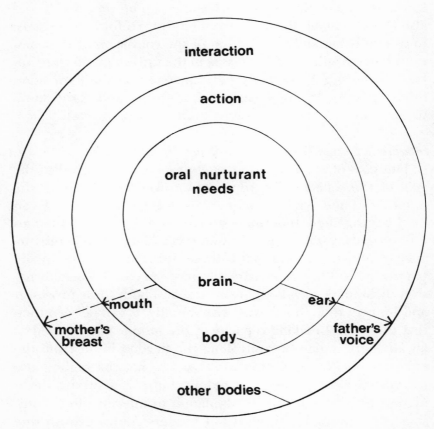

This diagram represents perhaps the nurturing interaction of a client with a cold, unresponsive mother and a warm, cuddling, humming father. In the deficiency of actual mouth satisfaction, the infant very likely found internal symbolic means (including thumb sucking) of satisfying himself; however, it is possible that those suspended interactive needs could also have been met by his father's frequent feedings, cuddlings, and hummings. This client may feel rejecting toward females, feeling that they are cold and unloving (and indeed he might develop a life style that would place him in the company of such females only) and may seek out warm men with a certain quality to their voices. It is clear what consequences such fusion and confusion can produce. Immediately the client's role in life is confused by having a father who is more mothering than his mother, a mother who is not a good target for affection, and a style of relating to males that includes receiving warmth from them—which style can lead receptively toward homosexual fantasies.

What we try to do with such a client is to resurrect the original pattern of interaction and then to try to bring to the mouth the sense of pleasure and satisfaction that the male voice brings to the ear. It is very likely that he will go through a period of rejecting the mother figure entirely, even though she is drawn as a warm, giving person and is played by a warm, giving female in the group. He will very likely have to reexperience and express some of the original deprivation, frustration, and rage at the unsatisfying mother. Once that experience and rage has been encountered, the way is open for the acceptance of the positive mother figure at some future time. The result of that series of structures can be a change in his self-concept and a change in his perception and anticipation of relationships with females.

Interactive Behavior Directed toward One's Own Body

So far we have only examined interactive energy that is fused or deflected from its originally intended target and seeks alternative targets in the environment. Now I should like to spend some time exploring situations in which the child finds the environment so impoverished that there are no relationships from which to draw alternate satisfactions. (Of course, if the parents

were physically abusive, the child could at least derive the "negative nurturance" described earlier.) This turning to one's self
is more fruitful in the area of protection and support. Let us
look at one possibility in the area of protection. As stated
earlier, the innate need for protection for the child is experienced as a wish to be surrounded by the strong arms of the parents. Diagramatically it would look like this.

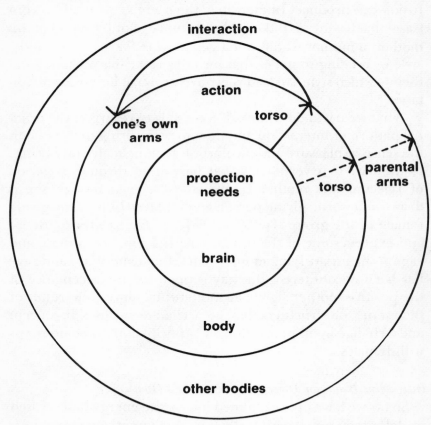

The dotted lines represent what would have occurred in the
natural, normal course of events and the solid line represents
what actually did happen. Certainly one wants a client to be
capable of protecting himself, but if he has never, or only rarely,

experienced the protection of his parents, it tends to minimize his ability to bring certain of his interactive energies in a more adult symbolic form into his contacts with other people. He tends to be aloof and self-sufficient, not needing people. A structure with such a client would probably include much rejection of the offers of help from accommodators in the group. If he were seen holding himself, one could speculate that the charged area of contact would be the surface of skin between his arms and his torso. If one could get him to relate those areas to others in the group, representing good parents, one would be well on the way to solving that bit of truncated energy expression. However, if one *assigned* such a client to hug his good parents, it would show some interesting results. Some clients who have been in such a situation have held the good parents with their arms only lightly, and the parent figures have reported that the client seemed to be shrinking away from them. Other clients have very strongly grasped the good parents and it soon became apparent that they were falling into the role of protecting the good parents rather than being protected by them. Still others have embraced the good parents so forcefully that they caused them to feel real pain. Possibly such a client was expressing, without necessarily knowing it, anger at the original set of parents and that is the assumption we would make in handling the structure. The leader could point out that the force directed toward the positive parents should indeed be directed toward the negative parents and should the client be prepared to express directly that anger it would open the door toward the future acceptance of protection from the good parents. At some point the client would probably have to experience or reexperience the lack of protection in the original setting. The feeling of vulnerability in the presence of the good parents would go far toward permitting that client to be vulnerable in a reality setting.

This particular structure outline points out how psychomotor therapy can split the ambivalence toward target figures and permit the angry feelings the client might have felt toward the good parents to be polarized toward the negative parents, allowing a successful acceptance of the positive input from the positive parents.

Clients who are represented by the diagrams showing the interactive energy being placed on inappropriate symbolic alternative figures and on inappropriate symbolic aspects of their own bodies can be classified, generally, as normal neurotics. Of course there are not hard and fast rules in this as people are so flexible that in some aspects of their personality they show pathology and in others they show complete normality.

Interactive Energy Shunted toward One's Own Mental Processes

Interactive energy is at first behavioral and then, as it matures with the individual, it becomes more symbolic. There are those individuals who by natural constitution or by devastating nurturant circumstances never experience their interactive energy—muscularly, motorically, or behaviorally—in sufficient doses for them to be able to utilize it as a normal part or their living process. A crude example of those circumstances might be a parent who constantly interrupted the child's normal interaction with her and the environment with admonitions and sharp noises or punishments. This could result in the child's not daring even to experience his interactive energy as a potential for action. Schematically speaking then, he would have to find some way to shunt his behavioral interactive energy to some "bodiless" system in his mind such as described earlier in dreaming, or to some symbolic system such as thought or daydreaming. Certainly this would not be a conscious decision but the results would be nevertheless decisive.

The extreme resultant of this would be the psychotic individual who had never properly made the transition from concrete behavioral interaction with a benign environment to maturation as a symbol-using adult interacting with the environment. The schematic design for such an individual would be as follows:

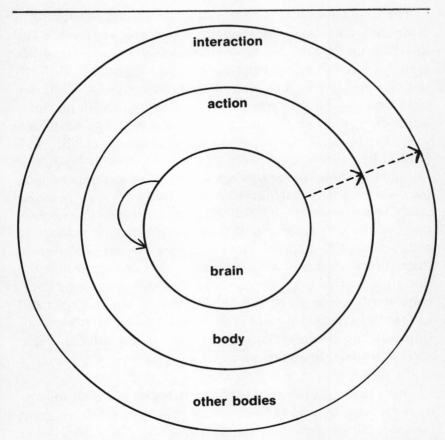

The dotted line represents the normal pathway for interactive energy and the solid line what occurs with those individuals who can be classified as psychotic or having psychotic aspects to their personalities. The body is left relatively untouched by interactive energy and the interactive energy amplifies the internal processes in the brain to an extreme degree. If this were a diagram of a battery it would be demonstrating a short circuit. In an analogous way it could be said that the heat of anxiety could represent the misdirected interactive energy in the same way as the heated wire in a short circuit represents electrical energy that has not been "used" for its intended work.

The interactive energy in this diagram is used as substitutes in dreams, hallucinations, thoughts etc. People represented by this diagram tend to have those characteristics described earlier as motor difficulties and behavior of bodiless type. The difficulties of working with this type of client are obvious. First, one must find some way to relate with the client although his interactive energy is not directed at one! Secondly, one must find some way to locate the target or targets to which it is directed. If the interactive energy were to reach the client's body, one would have some clue as to what was felt. But it is not reaching his body and it is reaching his mind, using his own personal symbolic processes. One must endeavor to decode the symbols that are the target for the energies and somehow manage to get the client to express those energies directly. Expressing them directly was probably so painful and even impossible the first time that getting him to do so now, so many years later, is obviously going to be difficult. Certainly the therapist will have to be extremely patient in developing a long-term relationship with the client, making it possible for the latter to begin to trust sufficiently to feel safe with expression in the presence of the therapist.

These clients have never sufficiently tested out the range of their feelings, so it is to be expected that they will have great misconceptions regarding the force of their emotions. And since they have little experience in truly individuating from the universal, they have no sense of what is them and what is not them, making it possible for them to believe that their energy expressions would have world wide repercussions. Another way of describing these clients is to say that their energies have imploded as can happen to the energies of a star. It has been speculated that such stars are difficult to find in the heavens because even their own radiations of light and energy cannot escape the intense force of gravity that has been set up by the implosion. I believe that clients who say that they have no idea what they feel are unable to receive energy from their imploded interactive systems which would give even them a clue as to what was going on in their emotional processes. In these cases I have tried to find these psychic processes that represent the binding energy of the emotions and then attempt to carefully loosen them. One example of that is a client who compulsively and frequently tapped three times in sets of threes to offset terrible consequences. I attempted in that case to suspend momentarily and temporarily that counting and tapping process and then to help the patient direct the resultant trembling agitation toward me or the environment in an acceptable and accommodating way. I speculated that the trembling, in her ordinarily very frozen and immobile body, was the appearance of some interactive energy. If I could find a means of showing her that I could help her contain, control, and limit that energy, I felt that I could assist her in making a tentative relationship with the real concrete world. Those attempts did prove successful in some measure.

Since anything can mean anything else in a symbol system it becomes extremely difficult to find those important interactive energy symbols in a psychotic individual who is not inclined to share anything of his inner world with you. So called "normal" clients often have difficulty in knowing exactly or entirely what they are thinking or really feeling in certain situations, and the process of making the interactive energy and expression explicit, concrete, and then accommodating to it simplifies the matter considerably. Perhaps this illustrates the difference between how resistance is met and handled in psychomotor therapy and how it is met and handled in traditional psychotherapy. In traditional psychotherapy the client is treated as if he is greatly interested in avoiding the painful process of therapy, and he must be goaded or pushed along by the therapist, implying that the healing force is mostly in the therapist and very little in the client. I find myself resentful of that implication. It makes the therapist too different from the client; granted that he is the expert and the client is in need, the client does want to feel better and get better as well as avoid the pain of his unhappy state. It seems that the therapist can assume there is operating in the client a normal health-seeking process which he can assist. Just as the medical doctor does not actually heal, but helps to set the natural healing process in action or to remove the obstacles to the natural healing process, so can a therapist understand that he is not actually the healer, but the assistant to the innate, balance-seeking mechanisms of the psyche.

When the psychomotor therapist offers the client the contract of accommodation he apparently also changes the rhythm of the therapeutic process as regards resistance. The psychomotor therapist offers an outlet and an accommodating target for the interactive energy that might be bound in some symbolic system. I can understand the difficulties clients in traditional psychotherapy have in the verbal situation where there is no contract for accommodation. In the traditional therapeutic setting the most painful memories of frustration, deprivation, unexpressed love, and anger are recalled where there can (by the very nature of the process) be very little response and certainly no accommodation. What are they to do with the activation of the interactive energy that such recalling inevitably produces? They must swallow it again just as they have in the first instance and added to that pain itself is the pain inflicted on them by their therapist who is reminding them that they are resisting. Once they have a place or arena, as they do in a psychomotor structure, to play out those feelings in an emotionally satisfying way, they are much more likely to face the issue of why they took such an indirect pathway to goal seeking and expression as they have done in the past. They will be in a more clear-headed and less painful position to explore alternatives to their behavior. Certainly many patients and clients in traditional psychotherapy do get help and do feel better after being in therapy; however I do believe that the process can be accelerated and significantly changed by the addition of some of the techniques being spelled out here and bringing to traditional therapy another set of tools and techniques to add to its already impressive armamentarium.

Resistance of a kind is met in psychomotor therapy. Some clients, at some point in their growth, do need to be goaded or pushed or reminded of the goal of therapy, but not to the extent that it is at the center of the process. Given a more satisfying alternative, most clients would opt for the healthier mode, just as would most therapists. However, on a scale that ranges from psychotic to normal, it is the patients with psychotic processes who show the most resistance in psychomotor terms. Those patients who have had a paucity of satisfying interactions are least inclined to open the old wounds; they have become rigidified in their pathological symbolic style of living.

Locating Interpersonal Interactive Energy in
Other Energy Systems

As discussed earlier, the interactive energy may find alternative routes for expression if the original, normal, archetypical pathways are blocked or not available. To repeat, interactive energy is essentially motor as well as oriented toward specific external targets. When a client in a structure stops moving and interacting with his accommodators, I hypothesize that there has been an energy shunting at some psychic level and, to locate it, I use a model of energy arenas with the following schema. There are five energy arenas or outlets, the one that we have been exploring being the interpersonal interactive.

The interactive energy of one arena that is shunted to any other arena can overload systems not designed to use that energy and becomes an indirect form of expression. Thus one who is not very active on an interpersonal level may be found to be doing a great deal of daydreaming and fantasizing or he may have myriad body aches and pains which take up a good deal of his attention.

I am not saying anything radical or new here. It is common knowledge that some neurotic patients will develop psychosomatic ailments and that some neurotics will be compulsive procrastinators and daydreamers. What is different is postulating that the energy they are diverting is interpersonal interactive and then giving those patients or clients the opportunity to redirect the energies in a controllable, satisfying, motor way, as in a structure. The discovery of the covert means of expression is not as important to me as the subsequent opportunity for the direct expression of those energies. In other words, insight is not enough. The insight should be the first step toward redirection, not only in the therapeutic session, but in reality.

Interpersonal Interactive Energy Shunted to the Verbal-symbolic Arena

Let us say that a client is in a structure, perhaps just having given motor expression to a great deal of anger at the negative mother. He now begins to lie in the lap of the good mother and may say that he wants to see what good nurturance feels like. He may curl up in the arms of the good mother and having seen many other clients nurse on a fleshy part of the accommodators arm or hand, attempt to do the same. Suddenly he may grow quiet and the expression on his face is such that neither his hands nor his mouth nor his entire body is energized in the usual and discernible interactive way. He is not being actively rejecting of the good mother; it is more as if she were not there and the client were not there. After some moments of such silence I would usually interrupt the client and ask what his thoughts were. Invariably they highlight or are associated very strongly with what has just been going on. It is an excellent opportunity for discovering the client's symbols for nurturance and for having the client learn his nonmotoric symbols for nurturance. One client at this point mentioned that he was in a kind of reverie about nature and particularly about trees and the woods. He recalled that as a child he loved to go walking in the woods with his father, and that as he grew older nature and woods were an important part of recreation and he spent a great deal of time camping and tramping out of doors. As a matter of fact, at this very time he was carrying in his jacket pocket a book on nature that he was reading in his spare moments.

The conclusion that I am drawn to in this case is that the client receives nurturance in a motoric way by being in contact with nature and trees and in a symbolic way by reading or thinking about trees. The stereotypical way of receiving nurture from a mother through his mouth was relatively meaningless to him at this time and any attempt to force it to be meaningful without engaging the energy around the nature symbols would be negatively productive. What I suggest the client do at this time is to fantasize that he is indeed in the woods or that his good mother is Mother Nature herself and to let himself experience the quality of emotion he gets in the presence of trees. He may walk, feeling himself amongst the trees or he may lie down feeling himself out of doors in the woods. One way or another, an attempt is made to reexperience the motoric aspect of the satisfying experience and then to try to associate that quality with the experience of lying in the good mother's arms. One step would be for him to attempt to hug the mother or relate in some way to the mother while thinking and feeling the way he does in the woods. He can be reminded that mothers can make people feel just as relaxed, safe, and at home as woods do. This is not to take away from the pleasures of the outdoors, but to bring that client closer to the possibility of relating warmly to females in a nurturant situation, first in structure and then, later in reality, in a peer relationship.

Also, the phallic aspect of the trees and its relationship to the father might be a possible association for the client. It is important to keep in mind, and to work with, the client's own associative processes, and not to press potential or future associations too early. With the knowledge that his love for the woods could include some aspect of making up for nurturant deficits, the client can review his emotional and experiential responses to females and see if they include, either in the present or in the past, the intensity and the quality he recalled while trying to nurse in the good mother's arms. If the client cannot successfully include the mother without doing injury to his sense of wonder and awe at the woods, it may be suggested that other group members stand and be representative of trees and then permit the client to "free-associate" in motor terms and see what he would do with the trees.

Similarly, another client found that nursing from the mother was a relatively meaningless event, but that the quality of the sunshine coming in the window had an uncanny attraction for him. By using the combination of his sensations in reaction to the sunshine in tandem with his relationship with the mother, he was able slowly to experience the lifegiving forces from the mother that he derived from the sunshine.

Other clients, when questioned about their silence might report that a word just kept going through their minds without attachment to anything that they thought relevant. The word, when spoken aloud and in the context of a nurturant relationship, might suddenly take on new implications to the client or the therapist. Clearly, the process of free association is rich for therapy; however, it is by the inclusion of the motoric element that another value can be reaped. To repeat, it is not sufficient to know, but the knowing as a focus for new action and a new relationship in the therapeutic setting can take the learning one step further. To include the motorically interactive process of psychomotor therapy with the associative process of traditional therapy is another way of describing the above.

Let me give another kind of example. Let us say a client feels that he is very angry and wishes to feel murderous toward the negative parents. He may set up the negative parents in front of him and have them tell him some of the negative things his real parents might have said in an attempt to arouse the heat of his anger. He may stand there, listening to the negative parents' insults, but not showing a sign of being angry; his body can be observed to be unenergized and quite relaxed. One thing that could be happening is that the client is absorbing the negative stimulus as negative nurture in the form of a humiliation feast. If that is the case it is important that the therapist intervene and stop the negative intake. Of course the therapist should tell the client why he intervened and that could lead to the client's new understanding of his unconscious attempts to manipulate situations to produce humiliations for him. It could also be very provocative to the client and he may be incensed at the interruption from the therapist and insist that he be permitted to "run his own structure." The therapist must use his judgment in this case and decide whether to allow the client to continue (for indeed he may be working himself up by the repeated negative stimuli to getting extremely angry) or to demand that the process be stopped.

I have learned from the times when I have been more permissive or lenient in cases where the client for long periods of time had not reacted to the insults heaped upon him by the negative parents by rejecting them or the content of their remarks. In accepting the insults from the negative parents, those clients seemed to be swallowing the negative input while building up an unexpressed feeling of hostile omnipotence. I learned to recognize that process and to demand that the negative input be stopped and that the client find some way to discharge the rage that was being built up in him. In fact, the term and indeed the concept of negative nurturance came from just such clients. Let me focus on the result of continued restraint or inhibition of reactions to negative stimuli. I have come to understand that result not only as a passive-aggressive device but also an an omnipotence-seeking device. I have hypothesized that all unexpressed or untested strong reactions are contained interiorly as a way of inflating one's fantasy sense of power.

All unexpressed emotions seem to amplify the longer they remain unexpressed. Those emotions need the testing of reality, and the limit-setting function of the good parents to place them in their proper perspective.

When such a client is asked what he is thinking about, he may answer that he was visualizing or fantasizing a tornado and that his parents were being picked up off their feet by the force of the tornado and thrown about. Saying this aloud might make the client laugh in delight at the thought. The therapist can suggest that the client imagine or pretend that he is the tornado and that he should express his interactive energy that way (yes, anger is interactive). He might then whirl about with tremendous energy and take great delight in the expression of it and at the accommodation by the negative parents. Or he might be appalled at the thought of getting angry at the negative parents and say that they are so much bigger than he that they would overwhelm him and smash him if he were to express anger. He could imagine a tornado knocking them about but certainly he could not imagine that he as a little boy had the power to affect them in the slightest. Perhaps his fantasy of the tornado was one way to offset the impotence he felt in their presence.

The goal for both these reactions is the same; to bring the interactive energy to the body itself and to experience either the accommodation or the limit-setting that would seem necessary and appropriate. Let us first take the reaction of the client who enjoyed being the tornado and enjoyed seeing his parents flung about by his force. It is good that this client is able to "muscularize" some of his anger and actively express it, but another step must be made. In being a tornado, there are elements of omnipotence and superhuman strength that would seem to need limit-setting and clarification. In fact the client who was able to become a tornado in this structure might find himself in the same condition as the one who could not imagine being actively angry at his parents even as a tornado, although as a human boy he would attempt to be directly expressive of his anger at the parent. If the therapist were to suggest to the tornado client that he express his anger as a boy, the client might find that he was feeling fearful and wanted the protection of the good parents. He then might tentatively poke a fist out toward the negative parents from between the bodies of the protective good parents and see what effect it had on the negative parents. If that were successful he might become more daring and then become more forceful.

The structure might take another tack. The tornado-acting client might become fearful after seeing the effects of his force and would find his anger vanishing while verbalizing that he is concerned about the fact that he has such violent inner feelings. The therapist could then suggest a limitation structure. The client could then vent the entire force of his anger and see that he could indeed be contained and this would be very reassuring. It should be clear that it is not a simple matter that we are discussing. When the symbolic forms of anger or other forms of expression are discovered, the client and the therapist must work toward finding situations that will tend to release the emotion and permit its expression on a motoric level. It was not without reason that the expression was symbolized in the first place. After the limitation structure, the client might find himself more able to vent his anger on a normal day-to-day level. There is a delicate series of judgments that a therapist in psychomotor therapy must constantly be making: whether to provide accommodation for the anger while having it directed toward the negative parents or to have the anger limited while directed toward the positive parents. The general rule of thumb is: if the accommodated anger produces fear or a sense of omnipotence, then limiting is in order; if the accommodation produces relief and a sense of being rid of the negative effects of the bad parents, then no limit need be set.

The client who could imagine the tornado but could not permit himself to behave like a tornado could be given a few alternatives. He might be offered or ask for the protection of the good parents and then have another group member behave like a tornado while he watches. Or he could have the good father behave like a tornado while he remained protected by the good mother. The latter alternative might produce other consequences. It might isolate him from the father and remind him of being fearful of the father while being protected by an over solicitous mother. Every move in a structure has consequences and a therapist must be alert to all of them.

Or he might want to behave like a little tiny tornado while in the protection of the good parents. He might begin with short puffs of wind and watch the effects of that on the negative parents. This could lead to a slowly rising crescendo of force until he finds himself able to more fully express his anger. Whatever alternative is selected, it is important that the client arrive at a place where he is able to express his own feelings effectively without relying on the protection or assistance of outside figures. Naturally, a client does not begin at that point but reaches it by slow degrees; using the imaginative and creative capacities of the therapist as well as his own, he can learn to find those avenues of expression that are open to him and develop competency and daring through slow developmental steps.

Whatever choice is made, the therapist should watch the effect it has on the client for only that way can he be sure that the appropriate moves are being made. Sometimes an alternative can be offered that makes remarkably good sense to the therapist and to other group members but which is a colossal flop when applied to a specific client. Only the client's reaction should be the guide to what is working and what is not working. Every new condition or element that gets introduced into a structure has consequences and some of the consequences can be absolutely unpredictable. Some minor move in a structure might remind a client of something with the most profound implications which cannot be ignored but must be dealt with. The client and the therapist must work in an improvisational frame of mind and dare to walk into the new territories that may be opened. One cannot plod along in a stereotypical manner, expecting that each client's response will be predictable. Primitive emotions may be stereotypical and one of the aims of the therapy may be to reestablish typical pathways for behavior, but each human being is remarkably complex and different from each other human being in terms of actual experiences and symbolic formations. The therapist should respect those differences and be prepared to respond to all the subtle changes and nuances of each client and of each structure.

Interpersonal Interactive Energy
Shunted to the Metabolic-vegetative System

Sometimes in a structure a client may find that he does not feel any impulse to move in any particular way, feels no tensions in any muscles and has no associations that are calling attention to themselves, but feels a pain in a particular part of his body, for example, his eyes. The location of the pain seems to have some relevance to his emotional state. However, that fact is usually learned after the exploration of possible movements pertaining to the pain and not before. For instance, the client might be in a structure or situation where the anticipation was that he would be angry. He does not feel angry, nor is his body energized in any way except for the pain in his eyes. At such times I have suggested that the client attempt to express the anger with his eyes—to try to pierce or penetrate the negative figures as if knives or a ray of some kind were coming from his eyes. The accommodators are instructed to respond to the subsequent narrowing of the eyelids as if they were being penetrated by knives or by a painful ray of some kind. The narrowing of the eyes and the accommodation sometimes seem to "connect up" in the client's mind and he feels that indeed his eyes are causing pain in the accommodators with their efforts. This can lead to an amplification of the expression and a slow shifting from the symbolic arena to the active. The aim is to bring the symbolic—and this time metabolic-vegetative—expression to the realm of skeletal muscular expression. Once again it is usually those clients who have found that their skeletal muscular methods of expression were either inhibited or rendered ineffective in their childhood who turn to these more symbolic forms too early.

Our aim in psychomotor therapy is not to make concrete primitive monsters out of symbolic complex humans, but to expand the range of expression in those individuals whose expression was not permitted to take the usual concrete course before going through the process of symbolification.

Significantly, during the use of the eyes as a weapon, the client often speaks of feeling as if energy were flowing from his eyes to the accommodator's and says that he is getting a great deal of satisfaction from the forceful narrowing of his lids. Frequently, the energy of the narrowing seems to travel to the rest of the face and a grimace or a tightening around the mouth ensues. Sometimes the client, as he experiences the rising of his angry emotions, begins to growl in an animal-like fashion. The growling can change to shouting at the accommodators and that can lead to the making of fists and the pounding of some object while the accommodator responds as if struck.

Often, after such a structure the client will mention that the pain in his eyes has subsided or gone away entirely. Parenthetically, it is quite common for a client to mention at the outset of a structure that he has a painful headache and following a successful and energetic structure report that his headache has gone. These comments have confirmed my belief that the interactive energy that normally would have led to a satisfying motoric expression had been shunted to another system. The pain in the eyes can be understood to result from an overload on that system.

Sometimes pain will be noted in the hands. In that case the client is instructed to motorically "free associate" and see what type of behavior, using that part of the hand that is in pain, and what kinds of responses from the accommodators provide a satisfying or pertinent feeling. It is possible that the client may wish to hold onto the hands of his positive accommodators and recall a time when he was very frightened and had no one to turn to. It is also possible that the client might find that when he made a fist with the hand that ached, a sudden surge of energy would flow into the hand, making it close into a much tighter fist. Or perhaps the client may want to strike at some object with the flat of his open hand. It is up to the client and the therapist to use their imagination and creativity in explorating the possibilities of the potential expression.

Sometimes a client may feel nauseated in the course of a structure. The way we have become accustomed to responding to that in psychomotor therapy is to suggest to the client that he permit the feeling to become active. For such occasions a large plastic bucket is kept available and many clients will go through violent and forceful retchings with the negative accommodators responding as if being vomited upon. The surprising thing about such expression is that no one has ever really thrown up in a structure more than a bit of phlegm although the feeling of the nausea is intense and the expression of it total and forceful. However I do not trust being without an available bucket in such circumstances.

The nausea seems to take two forms. Sometimes it appears to be a result of rage that has found that avenue for expression and other times it seems as if the client were attempting to get rid of an emotion that is an integral part of himself. If the latter seems to be the case, the therapist can mention that all his emotions are all right and that he doesn't have to get rid of any of them. This is an important factor, and if the client seems to respond favorably to that license to feel, it is preferable that the license come from the good parents. When the good parents say it, the client may remember that his own parents would not permit such expression and the structure can be polarized around the negative parents telling him to stop behaving in that fashion.

Another type of the seeming somatization of expression is suggested by the tingling that some clients report in various parts of their bodies. Wherever the tingling takes place, the client can attempt to move that part of the body until he comes across some movement that seems to be relevant or meaningful to what has been going on in the structure. (It should be noted that there are times when such exploration proves fruitless and the structure seems to become bogged down in speculation, both verbal and nonverbal, regarding what the client is really feeling.) The tingling is treated as if it were a way the body used to call attention to a portion of itself. I know that that sounds like a mind within the body talking to the watching mind of the client but, that is my anthropomorphic/poetic way of describing that phenomenon.

Sometimes the pain will show up in the chest or throat. Experience has shown that this tends to be a precurser to a form of expression that will include the powerful breathing of the client. This can result in structures with great shouting or great sobbing depending on which way the structure develops. There have been times when I have suggested to clients who have reported pain in their chests that they try shouting at their negative accommodators. If attempted when that is not the actual cause of the pain, the fact becomes obvious to both client and therapist. The client who attempts to shout when shouting is not the business of the body at that time, shouts with little force and expression. He may then adopt a relaxed exploratory stance, called a *species stance,* in an effort to find out what other kinds of motoric or premotoric messages there are in his body. What I am getting at is that the client may find that he wishes to cry and then remembers an event recent or past that has been weighing heavily on him. The resultant tears and sobs are not contrived but have, I believe, a direct relationship to the pain felt previously. For following the outbreak of sobbing the client often mentions the lessening or absence of the pain in his chest.

To sum up this chapter, the therapist in psychomotor therapy includes in his functions that of "tracking" interpersonal interactive energy. That is, he can see where the energy shows up on the body, help it to become concrete and motoric, and help to direct it toward appropriate targets. If the energy does not show up as overt action, his function is to find its symbolic expression in the realm of thought or fantasy and to assist in translating it back to action. If the energy shows up as pain, somatic disturbance, or tingling, he must help to translate it back into action and to clarify its expression and target. This schema of interactive energy and its possible conversion to other forms of energy systems, although hypothetical, provides a useful frame of reference when faced with the infinite possibilities that each human being in any situation presents to the onlooker. Previous to the use of such schemas, the work was more difficult and the learning process similar to groping and probing in the dark. Without such schemas, the description of complex events would be without shape or organization and without guiding principles to assist in the handling of the emotional phenomena of psychomotor structures.

Of course the schema alone is not enough. People are too complex and human and varied to place in *any* mold, however flexible. Not all phenomena are explainable by this schema, and moreover, even if they were, the therapist would still be faced with making all kinds of difficult judgments and decisions on a moment-to-moment basis and these cannot be made by any system, schema, or what you will. The therapeutic situation still demands the responses of a feeling, caring, intelligent, warm, and sensitive human being as well as a trained, rational, clearheaded, and thinking professional.

CHAPTER 5

Interpersonal interactive energy works through the emotional motor system, that motor system, described in my previous book, which makes people congruent with their feelings, emotions, and drives—a state which I call inner environment congruency. That is, it is that motor system which is impelled by the inner state of experience and directed toward a target. When I wrote about the emotional motor system in my previous book, I had not yet developed the concept of interactive energy and therefore did not realize that the matching of behavior to feeling could not be achieved unless the behavior resulted in a satisfactory response from the outer environment. For example, when one is angry with another person, his anger is resolved only if his movements effect a response from that person. Therefore I described it only in terms of that motor system that produced behavior related to interior states of feeling and being; paradoxically I described the voluntary motor system as that system that was utilized to develop congruency with the external world, not in terms of what one wished to do but in terms of what one could do to meet that world's demands. The effect of voluntary movement was not necessarily pleasure in the fulfillment of inner needs, but rather pleasure in the mastery of the body—making it do as one bid. Purely voluntary movement necessitates the inhibition of emotional movement and interactive energy. It is "learned" movement rather than genetic movement. By that I mean that the individual who gains mastery over his body and can move as the external world of objects and people seems to demand has learned to move that way by observation, trial and error, thinking, and planning. The person who moves directly to feelings in respect to his needs and his interpersonal relationships is using not so much learned movement (although the refinement of his primitive urges is developed by the addition of voluntary movement) but inherited movement patterns such as fight and flight reactions.

In the example of the structure where a client was active in an emotional way and then became quite still, and when asked what was he thinking responded with a verbal symbolic association, it could be said that he had shunted to mind energy; and if he were to move it would be sure to be voluntary movement. In fact those mental patients who have shunted their interactive energy from their bodies to their minds are most likely, primarily, to be using voluntary movement to activate and mobilize their bodies. Interestingly, voluntary movement can be used as a symbolic form of expression of interpersonal interactive energy. That is, when interactive energy gets shunted to the mind, not only does the mind provide symbolic expression of the interactive movement in terms of ideation and association but if the client were to move his body in the standard exercise of habitual voluntary movement, or voluntary patterns described in my first book, symbolic gestures and movement patterns relative to the interactive goals would appear.

For instance, if the client who had the ideation about a tornado were asked to move his body in a voluntary mode, he might very well perform some action that would be reminiscent or symbolic of the force, direction or nature of the tornado but without the energy, rhythm, and speed that would show up in interpersonal interactive, emotional movement. A person who was experiencing fear but who could not permit his body to move in terms of that emotion, would probably, without knowing why, select a series of movements or gestures suggesting protection, with the hands seeming to block a potential threat. Therefore, I see a connection between the symbol-forming capacity of the mind using words in mental energy and the symbol-forming capacity of the mind using the limbs and body parts in voluntary movement.

Voluntary movement is not to be seen as an auxiliary system for the expression of interactive energy, which it can be, but should be understood as a value in its own right. In the above example I am stressing only the aspect of voluntary movement that represents the spillover or shunting of interpersonal interactive energy to other systems of energy. Those other systems of energy have their own value and their own functions in the task of being a human, namely the capacity to control feelings and to respond rationally to and control the external world. Voluntary movement and mental processes of thought, symbol-making, ideation, planning, etc., can be understood as the highest and most recent acquisition of living beings that permits greater learning, memory, and transmission of learning for the purposes of adaptation and change in a rapidly changing environment. Those are the processes that are usually listed under *ego processes*. But I am not entirely satisfied with that terminology, and further on in this book I would like to develop my concept of self and the ego.

Concept of Identity

I understand the term *identity* in psychomotor therapy to include elements of location and orientation as they are understood in navigation. Identity then must deal with one of the same issues looked into earlier which is the process of individuation from the universal. If the goal of identity is to include the ability to locate one's self in time and space, one must be able to differentiate one's self from other figures in time and space and to differentiate one's self, more particularly, from the universal ocean of all other times and spaces combined. If one is identified with or unified with a universal flux of time and space, one does not have to face the issue of individuation and separation and location. One then *is* all things and all things are one's self. This is a stance that can be taken by some mental patients and can also be experienced under drugs. Some religions and philosophies seem to have as their goal the losing of one's self into the universal, but I feel sure that what they mean is to retain the capacity to lose sight of one's own individual self under certain circumstances and the capacity to see the universal relationship of all things. My preference is to be able to have an individual identity while seeing my place, and portion of, and relationship to, the universal.

The goal of identity seeking includes the idea of autonomy. That is, one's identity and location in time and space are more clear if one has the capacity to move one's self, feed one's self, support one's self, protect one's self, limit one's self, just as the womb primarily and the good parents secondarily did for one's self. If one is not doing those things for one's self, one must remain in a dependency relationship with figures larger than one's self who will provide for one's needs. One's location then must be relative to and perhaps a satellite of another body from which one never moves too far.

To have an identity one must have a finite shape; one must have boundaries and therefore limits. That is not to put man in a prison of rigidity—one understanding of being human is to be capable of "becoming," but even that potentiality must have limits. If there are places in one's personality where one does not know where one's self begins and ends and where others begin and end, one's identity is fuzzy. If one has interactive energy that has not been tested in concrete reality and found to have limits, one can have concepts about that energy that include its omnipotence and to that extent one's identity is fuzzy. Of course if one falls into the opposite frame of mind and feels that one has no power and therefore no range for one's efforts, that is another way of having no shape—or of becoming identified with the universal. One can thus see death and the loss of one's energy, form, and outline as a kind of merging with the universal. This merging with the universal can be reminiscent of the actual experience of the sperm merging with the egg and the fertilized egg merging, or more correctly joining, the uterine wall. Therefore those emotionally ill clients who speak of wishing to die may also mean they wish to recall or reexperience those earlier, probably very satisfying mergings and relationships.

Levels of Relating

I should like to digress briefly to discuss the point just raised. There are rising levels of relationship. The first level seems to be: merging or sharing of one's actual life place and energies with another, such as occurs in the act of conception. The second level seems to be: joining, as the fertilized egg joins the uterine wall and gains a flow of energy and life through it. The third: eating or consuming, as the infant eats or consumes the love from its mother through its mouth. Fourth: being held or supported or "understood" as one is tactually and then symbolically held up and touched by one's parents. Fifth: seeing, hearing, and speaking as one sees, hears, and speaks to one's parents and the rest of the world. Sixth: the sharing of information by symbolic means such as speaking and writing as one does in school and in the rest of one's life. Finally: the capacity to use the appropriate form of relating for appropriate circumstances including loving, marrying, and parenthood.

Certainly, one does not lose the capacity to relate on concrete, motoric, or tactual levels, but the capacity to relate on more symbolic levels does increase as one matures. Maturation must include, as mentioned earlier, the movement from the concrete to the abstract and the movement from the motoric or behavioral to the symbolic. Interestingly, however, many people manage to use symbolic levels of relating to satisfy earlier deficits of relating. For instance, those clients who may have a nurturant deficit and still need to relate by means of the process of consuming, may "consume" vast amounts of reading material and films, "consuming" aspects of the environment through their eyes. Other clients might constantly have to hear the voices of others in a manner that can be described as consuming the voices and sounds as if they were food and life sustaining. It seems as if all neural stimulation might be inter-changed for all other kinds of neural stimulation so that in the last resort, given the absence of all other satisfying kinds of relating, one can relate to one's self by giving one's self pain and at least having that to "eat." In the absence of satisfactory neural input on whatever level, we can always experience life so long as we can inflict pain on ourselves. My work with hospi-talized clients has shown me numerous cases where patients inflict wounds on themselves. Certainly there is an element of guilt involved in the process, but there is this self-nurturant aspect also.

Fixed Positions

To navigate, whether it be on the oceans or in the universe, one needs to have a fixed position as a point of reference. Sailors have learned to use the stars and the magnetic compass for this purpose. The young organism in utero does not need an external orientation point for he is not yet separate from one of his fixed positions. I have come to call those figures in human-identity processes who can be used as reference points, pole-star figures. It is important that these figures re-main fixed and relatively stable throughout the period that they are needed for orientation purposes. After the infant is born he feels the mother's physical presence and not only is that important in the nurture satisfaction the mother provides but also in the burgeoning process of identity-forming. It is as if there were two intensities of interpersonal interactive energy flow coming from the mother. One is the strong energy flow that provides for the living process itself. The other is a low-intensity energy flow or weak charge that is used in the process of orientation.

Respect

Respect, noted earlier as the fifth quality in the parental relationship to the child, comes into play here. Respect that parents feel toward the child can be likened to the weak energy flow that the child uses in his orientation process. Let me elaborate. As the child begins to nurse it has been noted that the child spends much time gazing into the face of the mother. The child can be understood to be fixing the image of its mother in its mind, that image being coupled with the pleasurable sensation and satisfaction of nursing. The mother tends to look back at the child and that can be translated as "I see you and you are good" in much the same sense that God in the Old Testament looked upon his works and regarded them as good. By that action, God proclaimed the existence and worthiness of what he had created and now saw as separate from him. It seems to me that individuation, separation, and identity cannot be completed unless some important figures proclaim that you do indeed exist, for they see you, and you do indeed have worth and are worthy of respect, for they have judged you. Before one can learn to withstand the impact of negative criticism in one's adult life, one must have gone through the experience of being respected and identified by one's own parents in a satisfactory way. One seems to need verification from the external world as well as from one's own senses that one is indeed alive and worthy of that right.

As the child begins to grow, and particularly as he begins to be able to move away from the mother, he must be able to return to the mother frequently to orient himself and to see if he is still there and still "a good boy" or worthy of respect. If his mother should be away for a protracted period of time, he would experience distress, not only because he will be missing her in the nurturant sense but because his still fragile sense of his own identity will be jarred. If she is not around he will become disoriented in a very real sense, like a ship with no stars and no compass to guide it. However, the child cannot be constantly in the mother's presence (and indeed if he is normal and has the child's normal curiosity, he will want to look at as much of the world as he safely can), and it is important that the mother be willing to permit the slow development of his autonomy in small successful steps. If he is separated from the mother too soon and too painfully it will be difficult to get him to dare to be out of sight of the mother for any but short periods of time. At first the child may need the actual touch of the mother to feel safe and locatable, then he may need only the sight of the mother, following that he may need only the voice, then perhaps the memory or the thought of the mother will suffice. Obviously there is a greater and greater abstraction and use of symbols in the process of orienting to the mother figure, reflecting the rising abstraction in the level of relationships noted earlier. I do not mean to leave out the function of the father in the identity-making process. As the child grows, the focus shifts from the mother alone to include the father with the mother. It is perhaps my bias in favor of the nuclear family, but I find it most important to have both mother and father present in the orienting process as early as possible. To find a third, unknown point it is well to have two known points. This helps the child distinguish between the different functions and roles of the two parents and aids him in identifying and modeling after the appropriate one.

As the child grows older, the father becomes more of the judge and critic and it is important for him to pass favorably on the production and behavior of the child. This favorable judgement should not be offered randomly or meaninglessly but should be appropriate to the level of the child's development. If there is no worth variation placed on the efforts of the child seeking approval, he will gain no satisfaction in his efforts to gain mastery over what he is doing. Without criticism or value judging, there can be no development of discipline, competency, or judgement, for without value judgments all things and all efforts would be deemed equal, and they are not. I do not imply that a child should be prodded constantly to excel, but I mean that values should be developed in the child. The relationship that I am describing includes the concept of limits. The child must learn that some things cannot be done and others can in order to give him a sense of definition and boundaries. The parents should assist in the development of values and limits for the child, but his support, nurturance and protection should never be made conditional upon his satisfactory production or behavior. The child's innate worthiness of love and care should be without question and without reference to his productions.

Interior Orientation and Identity Process

An analogy that I have begun to use in understanding identity processes is that of the interior stabilizing devices used in rockets in our space program. The equipment is so designed that the interior or onboard stabilizing platform is oriented toward certain stars and locked into that position. As long as that platform does not get knocked out in the sense of loss of current and so long as the onboard computers are fed information regarding speed and direction changes, the men on the rocket will always be able to find out where they are and can travel safely. I don't believe that the stabilizing platform has literally got to continue to see the star that it was originally fixed on. In a sense it has internalized the star or taken some symbolic, abstraction of the star and relates to it in its own interior. I believe that this is essentially what goes on inside a human child's head as he grows from the age where he needs literally to see the mother and father to where he can orient to them through his abstract, symbolic internalization of them.

In the process of growing older, the child becoming an adult begins to see beyond the parents and to search for other, perhaps ultimate, constant figures. Out of this search comes a seeking for God and a development of philosophies or creeds or world views which can be seen as constant and unchanging, much as one saw one's parents as constant and unchanging when one was a child. This search for constancy can be pathological as a result of an insecure childhood, or a healthy need for ordering the universe so that one can operate within it. The difference is in the intensity and capacity of the individual to find a satisfying meaning to life in general and to his own in particular.

It is also worth noting that as one grows older the constant figures one chooses are more likely to be symbolic and abstract like ideas and thoughts rather than concrete like people and places. I call those inner concepts *pole-star ideas* by which one arranges one's life. Just as one result of concrete, motoric interactions is development of the capacity for abstract, symbolic interactions, one result of having recognized concrete, pole-star figures is the capacity to use abstract, symbolic, internal means for orienting one's self. Just as the child who lacks concrete interactions can turn pathologically toward his inner processes to make up for the experiential deficits, so can a child turn too soon toward his inner symbol-making processes in an attempt to stabilize his disoriented and disorganized world. If he does so too early he will never have a normal identity, but more likely will not be able to differentiate himself from the universal because he is using a part of himself as if it were outside himself and therefore he must be "out there" as well as "inside here" in himself.

I have speculated that some of the clients I see in the hospital have learned to know who they are, so to speak, in their own pathological way by orienting themselves to their own anxiety. Here is how I arrived at such a conclusion. Let us say a child is removed too soon from its mother and feels the shock, disorientation, and distress that is a result of that absence. Let us say that that absence from the mother is continuous and that whenever the child looks for the mother, he fails to find her and hence experiences discomfort. I speculate that it is possible for that child to orient or know itself by way of experiencing anxiety over the absence of the mother. Paradoxically, if that client were not feeling anxious, I am not sure that he would "know who he was." Anxiety is chronic for some children and they may very well use it as a pole-star feeling. Some may say "I think; therefore I am." Others may say, "I feel lousy; therefore I am." Not only is it possible to survive with negative nurturance, but now we see it is possible to have a negative identity and still survive.

If it is actually the case that a client can orient by means of his own negative inner experiences and that he can nurture himself by means of his own negative inner experiences, how is one to bring the identity-making process back to the external world, and how is one to prevent the interactive energy from finding its target in one's own inner processes? That is one of the most difficult tasks I face in working with hospitalized patients. In order to become a parent substitute, a temporary pole-star figure, one must be constant and regular in all ways, and have the necessary patience to wait and find the means of interesting the patient in interacting with you in a way meaningful to him. There are some hospital patients who can see the therapist only as "friend" and cannot imagine him as anything else. If the patient gives up his focus on his own inner processes for identity and nurturance, he may literally die if there is not sufficient stability and love awaiting him. That is, he may kill himself in his frustration and hopelessness and rage. The patient's very life depends on this focus and he will not be careless in what he does. Even if he lives in an insane world by what he does, at least he lives.

The hospital itself becomes the limiting, nurturant, constant external object for some patients and leaving it may be very much like leaving the gaze of the loving mother. They may find it impossible to go away even if they have learned there to feel better. However, if a patient can learn to use the hospital as an identity reference point and as a source of nurture, the job of attaching that energy to the therapist and the group is a lot easier.

Working with identity concepts in psychomotor therapy is relatively new as most of our attention has been paid to interactive energy processes. Identity issues arise with feelings of disorientation and not knowing what to do or where to go. When such a quandary shows up in a structure, we have the good parent figures, standing close to one another, say something like, "We see you and we know who you are and we know you are good." Sometimes a client likes to hear his name mentioned in that context. It strikes me that early infant-identity growth includes four values: constancy, seeing or touching, naming, and approving or valuing (naming may include valuing, i.e., he made a "name" for himself). When the clients have said, "Tell me that you'll always be there," it has included more than constancy of nurturance and protection. When we have done "face-telling" (as described in my earlier book), we have been doing more than satisfying one's need for tactile interaction. Face-telling includes touching with a gentle, caring manner each part of the client's face, naming the part such as the eyebrow, eyelash, nose, ear, etc,; and saying that it is good.

There have been many instances of a client's asking to do a structure in which he makes something and brings it to the good parents for approval. Our experience has been that the client has wished for a reasonable response from the parent. Some of them have had parental responses that never included approval; no matter what they did, it never seemed to be good enough and they found themselves agonizing over every work effort with the dread fear that they and their work would be rejected. Other clients have mentioned that their parents said "good" to everything that they did and that it didn't seem to matter whether it was actually good or not, making it appear that the parents were not really interested in what the clients had done but were just brushing them off with a meaningless comment. Clients have let us know what it is that they wish to hear regarding their products by telling their positive parent figures precisely the words to use. Sometimes they wish to hear constructive criticism which they can then work on later seeking approval for the new end result. There seems to be a need for testing one's competency on a reality level without risking a crushing experience if one does not meet with instant approval.

As mentioned previously, it is important that the approval or disapproval not be connected with one's right to receive love, protection, etc. The valuing should refer to the product and not the individual himself. The individual himself is beyond measure and should be told so. What we are aiming for as an ideal situation or child-parent relationship is one which produces a child who is so certain of his intrinsic worth and of the constancy of his pole-star figures and concepts that he can attempt a new project without feeling that his very life will be lost if it does not meet with success. Naturally one does not meet with success in every new venture. New situations demand many trials and many attempts to rectify the new adjustments and refinements. Therefore, society must develop cultural attitudes and processes which prepare both children and adults to cope with the demands of a rapidly changing world.

One must be able to differentiate one's self from one's context (as the figure differentiates itself from the background). The tension of relationship between the individual and the context or between the figure and the background must be such that the figure is aware of the dimensions of the background, must feel safe in the presence of the background—that is, in an anthropomorphic sense, feel that the background likes and approves of it, is not hostile to it, or if it is hostile in some respects, that the figure can learn how to cope with or avoid the hostility. So what does the child need in relation to his context? One, a sense of the over-all picture; two, a sense of his separateness from the over-all picture; three, a sense of security within the over-all picture; four, a sense of self-worth, of his range of action within the context; five, a means of orienting himself to the context while he is moving and not only while static, i.e., of knowing who he is without having to remain still, or, to say it still another way, of not having his identity wrapped up with a location; six, the capacity to experience pleasure and joy within the over-all picture in sufficient degree to make the living worthwhile.

Identity issues, then, cut across a broad spectrum of other issues, including: individuation, autonomy, competency, self-esteem, capacity to symbolize the context, capacity to orient to symbols, and capacity to enjoy all this.

Changing Capacities, Changing Contexts

The difficulty of holding one's identity constant is that as we grow both our capacities and our contexts change. It makes it doubly important that our early identity-forming experiences have gone well for the later identity testings may prove to be too much for a fragile solution and the individual might very well become disoriented and unable to live should he face such a critical situation. Our present rapidly changing world compounds the problem by producing technological advances that have great implications for expanding man's capacities and for creating a shifting and uncertain picture of the total universe. The events of the world seem to be drawing a picture of man as an ugly, murderous, self-polluting, hateful, unnatural, immoral, corrupt, sex-obsessed, material-obsessed, untrustworthy beast, living in a world that was not made for him and that is hostile, dangerous, and ready to kill him if it gets a chance. A far cry from the idyllic pleasures of living in the womb and the perfect interaction between individual and context in that setting! No wonder people are having a hard time living today. This brings me to an absolutely crucial point in the practice of psychomotor therapy. How do we deal with the problems of the adult? How far can we take an individual in psychomotor therapy or must we forever keep him in a motoric, concrete, perfectly intermeshing, interactive system?

It has been adults who have come into therapy and happier, better functioning adults who have terminated therapy. We have been led by the adults to learning the needs of children.

We have not directed them to move in the manner in which they moved. Those behaviors simply flowed out of them. We only arranged an appropriate context for them. It is a fundamental role of the psychomotor therapist to assist in the development of a responding context to every act. The act is never performed in a vacuum, but always in a relationship or a context—this is my argument with any therapy which deals primarily with the intrapsychic. All behavior is interpersonal. There is always a figure and a background. If there is a blocking of intrapsychic energy, there may be body armoring in the individual which shows the location of the block, but that block was created in an interpersonal constellation and it will never do to manipulate away that block without dealing with the interpersonal element.

When adults come to therapy and behave as they do, seemingly regressing and dealing with ancient issues, are we to believe that there is some innate psychic balancing mechanism that is at work to show the client where the real problems lie, or are we watching a phenomenon of avoidance, resistance, and procrastination with respect to the real issues? My experience and the reports of my psychiatrist colleagues lead me to believe that the former is true. I believe that those people who in their present reality are seriously disturbed by the changing conditions in the world and who suffer impairment of their capacity to live are demonstrating the early fundamental, concrete, relationship failures of their past which are now bearing fruit. With the world as it is now, we must pay more and better attention than ever to our child-rearing practices. We have been able to get by in the past but that time is now gone. We can no longer permit the haphazard and unconscious development of psychological cripples that we have produced for thousands of years. Just as with the advancement of medical practice, we have learned to overcome and stop tolerating the obvious physical crippling and disease-ridden dislocations that had been taken for granted for long times past. We are all carrying about the pock marks of haphazard rearing. I know that that sounds like the attitude which seeks to put all responsibility on others, but I don't think that even the best of parents know how or have been trained to be good parents. Most parents have certainly done their best, but their unconscious messages and concrete motoric deficiencies—the good words and good attitudes notwithstanding—are what come through to the child. Our children are a result of what we do and not only a result of what we say or think.

We think that what we are doing in psychomotor therapy is a repair job on the past. Psychoanalysis takes us back to the past in order to review it, and see where the wreckage, bumps, and bruises are, in order to better understand the patterns of behavior that were a resultant of that past. That knowledge is available for application to one's present in order to improve the present and to eliminate negative patterns of behavior that were relative to the long-gone past but are no longer relevant. Psychomotor therapy attempts to return to the patterns of the past, not only through verbal symbols, subjective states of mind, and some somatic responses—as is done in analysis—but also through concrete sensory-motor behaviors and responses by which that past is "relived," on the assumption that when such concrete sensory-motor behaviors were originally aroused by the experiences of the past, they were inhibited and not satisfactorily expressed. Last but not least, psychomotor therapy attempts to provide those experiences and relationships that would have resulted in an autonomous, competent, self-esteeming person with a sense of his own identity. We do believe that it is possible to provide childhood-like experiences that are responded to in some ways just as if they had occurred in the past and are part of the client's history, but which would have better prepared him to live in the present. That is what I mean by a repair job on the past.

Clients who have gone through psychomotor therapy have reported to us that not only do they perceive the world differently and respond to the world differently and with greater competence and satisfaction but that they also perceive and treat their own children within the context of their new understandings. Psychomotor sessions are a good training place for becoming a parent. The learning comes from two directions: one, from experiencing motorically and behaviorally what one would have wanted in one's own past and understanding needs from one's viewpoint as a child, and two, from watching other people's structures from the vantage point of an observer or of a "good parent." One can learn from watching parent behavior in other structures or from playing the role one's self. Many clients have reported this to be a very important result of psychomotor therapy sessions.

Let us return to the question, "How do we deal with the problems of the adult?" I believe a partial answer has been given above. The adult does change his perceptions and patterns of behavior in the present, thus affecting his relationships in every sphere, including marital, job, and parental. However, there are clients who go through structure after structure, seemingly responding with strong affect in their movements and actions and seemingly coming up with new satisfying endings, who nonetheless remain in the same reality position in which they were uncomfortable in the first place. Of course psychomotor therapy is not always successful—in every instance and with every type of problem—but some of those individuals who seem unchanged by their work in therapy can be understood to have another frame of reference, usually symbolic, where they "really live" which they have not permitted to be touched by the therapeutic process. In these cases the symbolic frame of reference must be recognized and those interpersonal interaction energies that are bound within the symbols are able to be more fully experienced by the client. This permits that hidden aspect to be put into relationships with others. With those clients I have attempted to develop new techniques. The client in the structure is confronted with either the real figure involved in this problem or someone role playing the real figure rather than a polarized aspect of that figure. This type of structure is more like a psychodrama than psychomotor technique, but it gives the client a chance to practice directly those behaviors that he cannot seem to achieve in reality. If—in the midst of this psychodrama-like structure—an old pattern of behavior related to past events comes up, one can switch immediately to structures of the accommodating type or polarizing type and work out the problem through psychomotor means and then return to the reality setting.

Sometimes within a group there will be a reality interaction between members of the group or between a group member and the therapist. These are extremely valuable because there is no question whether a client is "play-acting" or pretending as there may be on other occasions. The relationship is permitted to work itself out on a reality base and often it will become apparent to them that there are massive projections from the past involved and this can lead to the development of a very meaningful and deeply experienced structure for a client who may have felt that many of his previous structures lacked these qualities. This kind of event points up very dramatically the relationship between the present and the past and gives the client an opportunity to work on present-day issues within the group with the same adults with whom he works out past-day issues. Some clients are so deeply concerned with immediate problems in their lives that they are uninterested in looking back into their past experiences for the answers they so painfully need.

Another solution that many of our clients take advantage of is concurrent membership in a traditional psychotherapy group, traditional psychotherapy one-to-one interviews, or well-supervised encounter groups. However, the expansion that is going on in the range of psychomotor therapy includes the use of the techniques described above. The hope is to make of the psychomotor group a multipurpose, multifaceted instrument that permits as much growth and learning as possible within the limitations of the time, capacities, and creativity of the group members and the group leader. Psychomotor therapy is not static but, it is hoped, is constantly developing and growing. My own active participation in many of my groups has permitted me the opportunity to grow in my own work and to observe the effects of my own changes on how I respond to the group and how the group responds to me.

Is the world a safe place to live in? Are we as a race and a species murderous and rapacious? Are we all partial schizophrenics not daring or not knowing how to interact with the world? Is the world a hostile, nonhuman, impersonal accident of random manipulations of matter? I think not. I believe that the interactive process does not stop being meaningful as soon as one leaves the concrete motoric world and enters the world of the abstract and the symbolic. We do not leave the Garden of Eden of our childhood as soon as we enter the world beyond people—the world of the abstract, symbolic, and impersonal. Or do we?

Two issues come to mind. One is the issue of interactive energy and its appreciation or meaning in the realm of objects and things in contrast to people. For I have discussed only interpersonal interactive energy, and have not paid sufficient attention to how man handles things. How much of his ability to handle things is innate and how much learned, and how much is his capacity to learn innate? The second issue is related to the first, having to do with man's orientation to or relationship with the total order of things beyond the usual sequence of environments within which he must find his place in order to have a solid identity. By *usual sequence of environments,* I mean the environment of the womb, followed by the home, school, the peer group, the job, the family which he and his mate head, and the society in which he lives. The umbrella under which all those interpersonal environments and relationships exist is the natural order of the entire universe. It seems that all cultures and all societies have at their base or at their pinnacle some mythology regarding man's place in the universe and in nature. All the other settings gain their meaning, or at least can be lived within in tranquility, so long as there seems to be some sense of total order in the material universe that includes man. The fact that all the rest of the universe visible to man beyond the universe of living things on this planet is material relates the two issues. There is some parallel meaning in the way we relate to the material world and the way we relate to the universe.

It seems to me that without a universal context, whether conscious or unconscious, overt or covert, realistically or unrealistically accepted or worked within, day-to-day transactions in the interpersonal contexts can break down. If one's world view is such that the natural universe is seen as hostile, and man as rapacious, how can one possibly live in tranquility? The fundamental issues of identity in our present time would seem to fall into two important categories. That is, the capacity to live well in any world would be enhanced considerably by, one, the infant's and child's successful experience of the motoric and concrete relationships that have been outlined heretofore, and two, the child's being introduced to concepts which cover the entire material universe and all its phenomena. Those cultures that still cling to orthodox beliefs even in the face of technological contradictions may have a better thing going for them and their offspring than have we in our knowledgeable but rootless and alienated superiority. The massive identity problems that we face in this era may result rather from the breakdown of the family and its capacity to provide concrete motoric interactional satisfactions and from the breakdown of long-standing moral, religious, and ethical universe-ordering concepts than from any rapid change in human-level contexts such as intensified schooling, job pressures, etc. Certainly those are important but their importance is dwarfed by the breakdown of more fundamental identity-clarifying processes.

It is hard to make even the smallest move unless one has some sense of the total picture. Without that there are no orientation points, no maps, no polar directions—just amorphous suspension of being. This may explain some of the behavior of some of our youth who seek primitive return to nature and /or powerful interactive, motoric release in sex and aggression. The recent phenomenal interest in astrology and transpersonal events points toward the need for some order that unifies our total experience and relates us to the physical universe of all matter and all stellar objects. The willingness of the two wealthiest nations on earth to spend vast amounts of money and natural resources on programs dealing with outer space may have more than a potentially militaristic value. Perhaps it is part of an unconscious search for meaning in the great "out there." Modern man's intense preoccupation with fathoming the secrets of the material universe by means of atom smashers and subatomic-particle research may be the natural corollary of exploring the universe.

It is becoming increasingly clear to me as I write and speculate that one of the tasks that modern man has to face (at least one of the tasks that I as a human being and myself have to face) is the finding of unifying concepts that make possible the total ordering of the material universe from the smallest particles of energies apparently without shape or form, through the natural world of living things—including man, built somehow out of the interrelationship of trillions of those particles—through the largest conglomerates of matter and matter-producing stars and galaxies. There is amazing order in molecular and subatomic structure. There is amazing order in nature and in man's own flesh and brain. There is amazing order in intergalactic shapes and rhythms. What is it all about? Where do we fit in? How did it happen? What do we do about it? What part do we play in it? What is our identity, our role in relationship to it all?

Must seeing all this boggle the mind? Does seeing all this banish one from the oft-mentioned Garden of Eden? Obviously it doesn't have to boggle the mind. Man is already deep into mysteries of the atom and of space and still going strong and wanting more. I think it does banish humans—or rather distinguishes humans from other animals. And it is just this step from the concrete to the abstract that does it. However, that does not mean that we must lose our capacity to live in the motoric and concrete. We can have the best of both worlds. It is not an either/or proposition though some might make it seem so. There are those who believe that since the highest order of evolution is represented by man's capacity to think, speak, and symbolize that he should live as much as possible in that higher order. Doing or believing anything that might remind them of lower orders would be to become less human. I am doubly reminded of the popular shock at Darwin's suggestion that we might be descended from or related to the ape and also of some analysts' shock at the possibility of a client's "acting out" or doing something other than verbalizing while in his office—both suggesting that such relationships and such behavior are less than human. Just because we have the capacity to build a tower on the Empire State Building, must we never descend lower than the eightieth floor or—heaven forbid—visit the subbasement?

Paradoxically, all this speculation about the value and meaning of the symbolic has originated out of my deep involvement in and understanding of the motoric. Even the Empire State Building had to have a foundation built first that would support a structure of great heights.

I would like to speculate about man's innate capacity to deal with the material universe. I have made a long case for man's innate ability to relate to other humans by means of the concept of interpersonal interactive energy and I submit, one, that there must be an innate base for man's obvious capacity to deal with the material world and two, that there must be systems of energy and relationship for such dealings which perhaps are connected to those already hypothesized. Material things obviously "know how" to relate to other material things. The order in the universe is sufficient evidence of that. The rising complexity of elements from hydrogen on up through the addition of electrons demonstrates that matter knows perfectly well how to relate to other matter and to develop greater and greater complexity of forms and properties as a consequence. Even our celestial bodies know how to relate to one another through gravity and probably other not-yet-known means of energy interactions. Since we are made up of the same particles that make up the material universe, we have on some level innate knowledge of how to relate to nonliving matter.

Recall that our rock (discussed in Chapter 2) knows how to hold all its particles together to form a coherent and conglomerate whole. Our tree is a master in doing what I have just wished a human to be able to do, that is, find its place between the microscopic and the stellar. Our tree, by means of its roots and with the help of water, relates to inanimate minerals and with the help of the far distant sun manipulates those material and energetic elements into its own life. Obviously then it knows how to relate to material and energetic things. (Watch that word *energetic* for I think it will probably return to haunt me in the disguise of *spiritual*). Our cat doesn't pay too much attention to material things except to walk over them, leap on them, and push them about a bit. Our cat and most other animals affect the world through their stomachs. Some animals such as ground hogs and gophers can relate to the material world through their instinctive ability to build nests out of material things. Other animals such as birds and beavers can manipulate living things such as twigs and branches and logs to make their homes. Most of the manipulations are done with the mouth and a little bit with the claws and paws of these animals. Most of the manipulations are made for the purpose of home building (context-securing and ordering?). The major way that the animal world relates to and affects the world is, I repeat, through their stomachs. By grazing, hunting, and foraging, the animal world changes the surface of the globe. By metabolizing what they take in and then by eliminating their wastes, the animal world affects and yet maintains an ecological balance with the world. It strikes me that metabolism is somewhat analogous to human processes of thought and symbolizing. Metabolizing includes the taking in of raw material, breaking it down to some of its component parts, the manipulation or reordering of those components, the use of the component parts toward the furtherance of the life of the individual, and the elimination of what is not or cannot be used. Human thought and other mental processes seem to use some of the same elements: the taking in or raw experience, breaking it down into associative components, the manipulating or reordering of those events, the use of portions of events toward the furtherance of the life of the individual, and the forgetting or discarding of what cannot be used.

Animals' primary mode of relating to the world can be expressed by the equation relating equals consuming. Humans can operate on that level of relationship, but can also add other modes that are analogous though on another level. This way of ordering things has some fascinating applications. It highlights the fact that all energy systems and all motor systems have an end result that is interactive and that the interactions are different in that they are operated on different levels of being: the reflex, the metabolic, the interpersonal, the material, and the symbolic. It points out the possibility of certain pathological ways of relating. Some mental patients relate on what must be the metabolic level, that is, the basic assumption is that the relationship is consumptive. For example, the cannibalistic thoughts of some patients can simply refer to the metabolic level of relationship or, relating is consuming. Other pathological modes of relating can result from using the mode in relating to material things and applying symbols to the interpersonal

EXPERIENCE IN ACTION   105

field—that is, treating people as if they were things and symbols rather than as people. For example, I have found myself treating my clients as if they were "cases" and not so much as if they were people. Obviously there are many varieties of pathology and many variations among relationships, but pathology can be seen as the application of inappropriate relationship modes, as in the above example of patients who treat themselves and everyone else as if they were inanimate objects rather than human beings.

We have not yet applied the metabolism metaphor to interpersonal interactions. Perhaps this level of interaction functions to take in relationships and break them down into their component parts for appropriate assimilation and use in the furtherance of life.

Humans, as distinguished from animals, have the capacity to interact with and to influence the material world, through the body in the form of voluntary energy and movement and through the mind by means of symbolic manipulation and the combination of the two. The combination of the two has resulted in the fantastic technological and industrial growth of the recent past. The mind manipulates material facts to create formulas as methods and decisions to be carried out by our voluntary motor systems or by machines. In this way, we are capable of complex and controllable behaviors having little to do with interpersonal interactions. The machine is an extension of the body for the symbol producing mind. What an interesting dilemma we humans are faced with. We are the first species that has found itself with the capacity to do this type of material exploration and manipulation, and we do not yet know the end of it nor even how to integrate it into the totality of our being—note the increasing complaint of the *impersonality* of our technological advances. It seems to me that the ultimate aim of our voluntary-movement and symbol-making capacities should be to place us in a more meaningful relationship with the material world from the subatomic to the galactic. It should permit us to manipulate the microscopic without losing sight of the ecological up to and including the universal.

This brings us back to the original question which produced all this speculation. What is man's place in the order of things? What is the greatest and primary context within which man must find his place and identity? From the preceding it is obvious that man is part of nature and is that part of nature that can see itself and the world and perhaps alter itself and the world in the direction of greater value to all nature. Man is nature becoming itself in the form of an individual. The processes of individuation, of autonomy and identity-seeking can be seen as a return to a religious frame of reference in which no aspect of life and living is without regard for and relationship to the universal order of things. Scientific and technological man is not antireligious so long as he does not become impersonal. If man can remain personal while fulfilling the highest order and capacity of symbolic and material controls and manipulations over the world, his every move will be in vibration with universal rhythms. Man does have an innate ability to interact with and to know and understand matter. And since matter is all that there is in the universe (I do not exclude the spiritual from matter), man can learn through his innate capacities to make a better interactive match with nature than he now has. I believe that the tool of symbolic control and voluntary manipulations is so new to the species and so relatively unpracticed that it is, so to speak, still in its infancy. Perhaps another way to explain the disruptive effects of the use of man's capacity for control of nature is to say that they are caused by the distortions in the symbol-making process by unfinished and poorly finished business on the human interactive level. If we were to perfect or at least improve the ways of providing for our human interactive needs and matches, perhaps the people that were a result of this could use their minds in a way that we have not heretofore seen, in the service of humanity and all living and material things.

Then the work of psychomotor therapy is thus applicable to the problems of the adult. It frees his adult symbolic energy capacity from the distortions of shunted interactive energy. It also gives the adult in a group the potential use of this frame of reference as a guide to his identity-seeking problems. If the parent figure in a structure saw the world as a good place, within which man was part of the natural order, the child figure in the structure would be able to face going out into that world with a little more equanimity than if the parent indicated the world was a hateful place and man a hateful creature. As an individual grows in psychomotor therapy, he needs less and less to do structures and eventually does not need to do them at all and leaves the group. If at times in his life he finds that some interactive-energy imbalances are showing up, he may return to the group for a one-or two-time participation. Or if he finds that his emotional energy is inappropriate in certain events, he may do an internal or "head" structure in which he will work out the energy dispositions in his mind as he did so many times before in an actual, concrete, motoric way. What I mean is that those who are successfully undergoing psychomotor therapy find that their everyday lives are becoming more effective, and when they are troublesome they explore the issues in a structure to see if they can be sorted out by using the models outlined. Thus there is an interrelationship between the real world of the client and the structure or psychomotor world of the client, with structures used as a kind of emotional kidney to clean misplaced interactive energy out of the everyday events.

I would like to mention here that many of the clients that come to psychomotor therapy are not emotionally ill as emotional illness is usually understood. Many are professional people who are quite effective in their respective areas of expertise. How is it that they have so much misplaced interactive energy? It is startling to me to work with a group of professionals in a workshop for sensitization to psychomotor techniques and find the great extent of unconciously learned mismatches in interactive energy. Perhaps it is because this frame of reference has not been used before that this is so. It is as if this process permits the wearing of a set of lenses that bring into appearance and into focus other aspects of our lives that were relatively hidden to us before. Therefore I see psychomotor therapy largely as an educational technique and not only as a therapeutic technique. In fact "normals" seem to be able to grasp its application more rapidly than neurotic or psychotic clients. But these terms are so flexible and overlapping as to become meaningless anyway.

There is still something nagging me regarding the identity issue and the universal frame of reference or context. I left the poor human being at a point where his mind either becomes the universal context or at least creates the universal context, both positions getting him perilously close to omnipotence and its consequent distortions and dislocations in feelings and interpersonal relationships. Let us then hypothesize further.

Let us assume that the innate structure of matter and energy is such that life as we know it can assemble itself out of extremely complex relationships—molecular, cellular, organic and interpersonal—and that all of these could be understood to be innately possible were one to know the inner structure of the atom of hydrogen and all its structural potentials—in the same way that chemists have been able to predict the properties of elements before they were found in nature. By all this I mean that the kind of evolution we have here on earth producing human beings can have gone on before in other systems and may be going on now in millions of star systems and planets. Those beings in other solar systems may be less advanced than we are, at the same level as ourselves, or much beyond our level of development. Until now, none of those beings has "taken over" the universe and controlled it for their own use or if they have the news has yet to reach us. What kind of control can they exercise on the vastness of space? What is the limit, what is the extent, that they or we can reach? My earlier point of conjecture left man at a point where all of nature was potentially under his control. If that were so what would be the relationship between us and those other creatures who are assumed to be so far advanced beyond us? Obviously we both would be only minute fractions of the total force and order of things since we were only the furthest possibilities in a set of, if one were knowledgeable enough of the possibilities inherent in matter, limited and finite possibilities. What if we had disagreements as to what would be the most valuable course of action we could take that would affect both our societies? Would they then have to destroy or control us or we them? Or would there be only a limited or singular set of choices that would lead to a better future? If the answers were limited, then where would man's freedom and control be? What would happen to man's free will? Man may be said to have free will to the extent that he is able to transcend his instinctive or interactive, interpersonal nature, but within the level of the symbolic, and the areas of manipulation of the material world by the symbolic, there must be some outer limit of possibilities and controls as there are in every other system. Or do we then rise to another system beyond symbolic and what would that be but spiritual?

Is there a consciousness and a responsibility for all levels of things from material through organic to animal to human to spiritual beyond man's, or at the very least beyond my own? For myself, I believe so. For I am tired of holding the world up and figuring it out for myself and perhaps for others. Surely there must be other human beings at work in this and surely there must be ranges of order and consciousness and control beyond what you or I and other humans on this planet can even conjecture about. I capitulate to those higher orders of consciousness and control. I and the world I see are less than a speck on an atom in a molecule of a cell of an organism that consists of all of the material universe. Or perhaps all the material of the universe is an aspect of the consciousness of that organism. In this context when we speak of God, how can we say that he "sees" us or that we "see" him. The best we can do is say that by some innate means beyond our senses we can experience the order and rhythm of the universe as we travel in it and it vibrates through us. We can never leave it or it us for we are but a small gathering of its energy coiled around itself, seeing and experiencing itself for a moment in eternity that for some reason seems to contract and expand. What is the point of being, then, if being is so short in pulsating eternity? The only answer that I can find in myself is that if I am part of the show, even for only an instant, I want to enjoy every moment of my own share of eternity and use every part of my portion of energy, action, consciousness, and responsibility that I can lay my hands on. I believe that as there seem to be an innate interpersonal ethic and interactions that can be discovered as well as destroyed in human life, there is an innate interactive ethic between man and matter and between man and the universe that can be discovered and responded to or not with consequences that can lead to order, meaning, and tranquility, or disorder, meaninglessness, and despair. I choose the path of seeking balances and interrelationships with matter, animals, man, and the universe that will lead to more productivity, joy, and tranquility for myself as well as for as many others as possible.

I would like to now go on to other aspects of psychomotor therapy including the concept of the ego in that process.

CHAPTER 6

My study of psychology and my work in psychomotor therapy have shown me how difficult it is to define the ego.
Sometimes it has seemed to fall under the category of controls and consciousness, sometimes under that of inhibition,
and sometimes it has seemed that the ego functions to give
us a consciousness of ourselves. I have believed the ego to
be a process that develops gradually in a person as he matures, and yet young children have exhibited controls and
consciousness and inhibitions which seem to contradict that
belief. At one point I thought that the ego was represented
primarily in what I call voluntary movement and that the
id was operating in what I call emotional movement. What
I have now is a set of concepts and processes that I loosely
lump together as the ego. Perhaps they will become more
defined as I write.

An analogy that has been helpful in my work is to describe
and understand one aspect of the ego to be like the skin
of the self, and in that respect to have a function parallel
to that of the skin of a one-cell organism. The skin of a
cell has the function or responsibility to hold in the matter
of the cell and to hold out the rest of the world. However,
it is not a matter of rigid control but of articulated surfaces
which hold most of the world out and let some of it in.
For naturally the cell needs to take in energy from the world
and to know in what proportions either to let that energy
get in or to pull it in. Thus the cell is a body of interactive
energy systems contained and regulated by its skin. Perhaps
the "ego" of the cell can be described as the interface on
the body of interactive energy where it comes in touch with
the world. Then in the human the ego could be seen as

the psychic equivalent of that interface on interactive energy. The ego or interface or skin must be able to recognize and discriminate between those things in the outer world it needs and those it doesn't need and to control the quantity and timing of the incoming energy, for certainly if it opened its surface to a certain nutrient for an unlimited period it would burst. Therefore the ego needs discriminating abilities and timing abilities, that is, some capacity to measure quantity, quality and time.

If the single-cell creature has a complex interior with different processes going on within it in various locations, then the skin surface would have to be articulated to take in certain nutrients in one place and certain others in another place. Obviously then it would have to "know" something about interior processes as well as exterior elements so that it could assist in a more perfect match between the interior and exterior. It would possibly even have to know about the interactions of certain interior processes for some of them might have the potential to grow faster than the skin and to cause the entire organism to burst and to "leak" out of its skin and become indistinguishable from the outside. Then the functions of the ego would seem to include "knowing" something about its own over-all dimensions and something about its capacity for flexibility. Therefore it would have to know the difference between itself and other things—would have an identity. That is, ego processes are included in what we have called identity processes.

If that one-cell organism were "born" full grown, so to speak, it would not have to go through any developmental stages and be sure that its ego was pacing the rest of the organism properly. It could also then be assumed that the ego knowledge and functioning would not have to be learned and were therefore genetic. The learning would have been automatically passed on by the "parent" organism. Therefore one can surmise that at least some aspects of the ego are inherited.

Let us now turn to the human. The ego problems for the human are compounded at once if we are to follow out the two new statements we have arrived at so far. One, that the ego can be described or understood as the interface between interactive motor systems and the outside world and, two, that there are five interactive energy systems operating in the human.

When is the ego born? That is an interesting question, for both the sperm and the egg are temporarily viable single-cell organisms with a membrane which must include an interface and therefore by our definition must include some primitive ego processes. To speculate with that assumption one step further back would lead to the postulate that the interfaces on merging or matching surfaces of atoms which were involved in a chemical change would include something like ego processes for the interfaces would have to be able to discriminate, to make measurements, and judgments in some perhaps mechanical way. Poetically, knowing (or ego) is on the surface of being and being is interactive energy. What is the material world if it is not interactive?

We must begin with one form of interactive energy that is potentially articulable into five systems with their variations according to the structures they energize.

The basic interactive targets are: gravity and the ground, food and air, people, things, and symbols. It is easy to see how these targets can overlap, and indeed one of the problems of life and ego growth is distinguishing them and relating to them properly.

Perhaps one of the reasons that the distinctions can be confused is that the systems I have hypothesized are not absolutely separated. The brain works as a totality within which there are structural differentiations.

The ego must distinguish between all those systems and the environments or targets with which they engage. When the egg is fertilized, the two primitive egos unify to become one. While the growing and dividing cells have not yet individuated into systems and varying functions, the ego must reside on the interface between the cells and the uterine wall on a metabolic or chemically interactive and discriminatory base. When there is sufficient mass and complexity to the foetus it begins to develop a reflexive motor system and therefore can respond to gravity. When there is sufficient cellular individuation to make distinctions between inner and outer, the outer skin surfaces must begin to develop sensory awareness and controls that are the beginnings of interpersonal and material manipulations. By the time of birth, then, the infant has quite a history of interactions: nine months of chemical, gravitational, sensory-motoric relationship with the mother via the womb. When the child leaves the womb, it has already learned to move its arms and legs, perhaps to grasp and manipulate the umbilical cord with its hands, perhaps to suck its own thumb, to feel the shape and limits of the womb with its head, hands and feet and all skin surfaces. When the child is born he is not complete and independent as was the one-cell organism in our original example. He still has a long distance to travel in becoming an independent, autonomous individual with a sense of his own identity. In other words the total person, or self, will learn or develop in the context of the world in which it finds itself. The organism and the ego can learn from interactions with the environment, ranging from chemical to behavioral to symbolic.

Although the child is learning about all five interactive processes simultaneously, there is an obvious developmental sequence that must be followed. While those higher developmental sequences are not yet mastered the child must depend on outside forces, namely its parents, to augment, complement and supplement its own still inadequate ego processes. I am suggesting that the parents, and at first particularly the mother, are to be understood as a neural or ego extension of the child. The ego, then, must be able not only to learn, but also to be somewhat parasitic or dependent on others while not losing its own potential for independence and autonomy. To some extent the ego already had such a relationship with the womb of the mother. Now, after birth, the relationship continues between the ego and the mother and father, and more interpersonal than the impersonal and chemical relationship it had previously. I begin with the relationship with the womb to demonstrate the continuity of slowly diminishing dependency on aspects of the environment that the child and the ego of the child experience.

In terms of the order of this book we are reexamining the needs of the child but now with the addition of concepts of the ego, interactive energy and identity process to ideas of memory, learning, relating, individuation from the universal, and development of the symbolic from the motoric. The orchestration and control of all these factors is under the responsibility of parents, teachers and society in that order. The parents' task of guiding a child's development so that he will be able to relate successfully to the world he lives in is an undertaking worthy of an artist of the highest calibre. The complexity and interrelationship of the various developing processes in the child must be monitored by a parent who himself is changing and growing at his own speed.

Let me quickly sketch out the process of sequential development of the ego of the child and then I would like to point out some hypotheses regarding ego malfunctions. The first task of the ego of the child is to gain, or rather to assist the interactive process to gain, a satisfactory and satisfying relationship and control over the metabolic and reflexive processes and interaction with the world of food, gravity, and ground. To put it more simply, the child has to learn how to eat, to control his sphincters in the process of elimination, and to master the skill of locomotion in a gravity field with the ground under his feet. All of this is learned in conjunction with reflexive processes that do most of the actual coordination. There seems to be relatively little that the ego must "do" in the realm of reflex vegetative interactive system besides deciding "when" to chew and swallow food, with a little addition of "how," and little else. While the infant is gaining mastery over this universe, the parent is filling in by feeding the child, cleaning up after him when he still cannot and should not be expected to control his sphincters, picking him up and carrying him about while he cannot yet walk.

As the child learns to do those things for himself, he gains a sense of accomplishment and a sense of identity from the approval he receives from his parents. If for some reason he does not succeed or is not permitted to succeed by overly solicitous parents, he suffers an ego distortion, an interactive energy distortion and an identity distortion. I point this out to show the complex nature of single events and the implication this has for the therapist.

If we return for a moment to the illustration of the ego as a skin or membrane around the interactive living process of an individual, then we see those parents who refuse to permit the child sufficient opportunities to develop his own ego insisting on remaining a part of the child's "skin" or ego neural processes. The child and the parent then can not separate from each other sufficiently to become autonomous individuals. The ego malfunction that the parent produces in the child is reflective of and complementary to the ego malfunction in the parent himself. Unless he succeeds in overcoming the infantilizing effects of the overly solicitous parent, the child is condemned to remain at the level where relating is still consuming and where his ego is not differentiated from his parents.

The next stage in the development of the child is his learning to control and master the realm of the interpersonal and the energies and behaviors of that interactive system. This stage presents the child with the opportunities and the internal capacities for achieving his interpersonal needs with his parents, his siblings and his playmates. His sexual and his aggressive energies come to the fore in this stage and he must learn to use them, limit them and control them with the aid of his parents. He is also still somewhat faced with his needs for support in a physical as well as emotional way, he still has to deal with nurturant and consumptive needs, but now in a more personal interactive way than in a primitive metabolic way. He learns then to distinguish between his mother as the deliverer of food and the food itself, and to see her as a person who provides him with emotional and personal satisfactions. It could be said that his ego in this stage needs to learn to discriminate all the various targets for his interactive and interpersonal energy. Without adequate ego discriminations his interactive energy would blindly attach to any and every target as it appeared. He must also learn to tap the full range of his sexual and aggressive energies and find their limits. It is most important that they be tested in concrete behavioral interactions.

The final stage of ego development deals with the handling of interactive energy which relates to material objects and symbols. This is the level at which eye and hand control, speech, creativity and value judgments are developed. This stage ties in with the producing and approving mentioned earlier in the identity process. The competency in work and in the manipulation of ideas and symbols increases one's capacity to satisfactorily engage in the world of objects and ideas and to gain mastery of both. Again it is the parent's job to help the child to engage in this growth and to help him make realistic discriminations regarding his efforts and his results. This process goes on throughout schooling and is overseen by teachers, religious figures and the society in general.

Ego Deficiencies

My experience indicates that if the parents have not done their job properly, the child does not complete the development of his ego and that he has, in a sense, a gap in the skin of his ego which permits too much energy either to flow in or to flow out. All deficiencies of interactive needs will be reflected on the developing ego. For instance, if the child is not permitted to develop his own capacity to support or protect himself, his ego will include the strength of others as part of his own interactive equipment. In the event that his parents go away or die while he has not yet acquired this capacity, he may undergo a great shock which can be experienced on three levels. On the ego level it can be experienced as a great rush of stimuli coming from the outside world which overwhelms him and which he cannot control or master. On the interactive level he can experience the frustration of an interactive need and know the pain and anger which it engenders. On the identity level he can experience the failure of his own competency and judge himself inferior and also experience the shock of the sudden absence of a pole-star figure which is severely disorienting. The parents, then, are not just "out there" to a child who is growing. They are also very much within his growing ego, and it is their job to see to it that the child learns to take over gradually in his own ego their temporary functions. This task, precisely what is undertaken in psychomotor therapy sessions, can be described as an attempt to satisfy interactional needs and to develop ego discriminations and controls, identity, competency and interior orientation positions by using the good parent figures, teachers and mates to provide the appropriate response at the appropriate time.

Some Concepts of Impotence and Omnipotence

The diagrams used on the chapter on interpersonal interactive energies shed some light on the processes of omnipotence and impotence as they apply to psychomotor therapy theories and practices. If the developing ego of the individual is described figuratively as appearing on the interface of interactive energy as it searches for appropriate and satisfying targets and relationships, it is possible to show how the egos and actions of the parents help shape or distort the ego of the growing child.

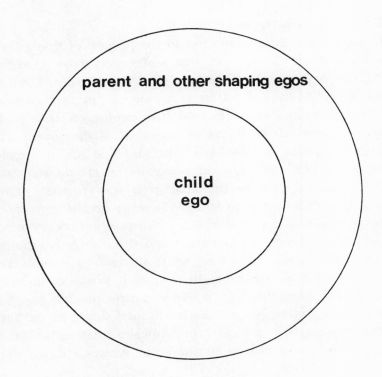

I must point out the limitations of such a diagram to emphasize the great variations that might exist within such a seemingly static relationship. For instance, the innate outward drives of the interactive energy are not shown here, nor is the potential variation of intensity of those drives due to genetic factors. By that I mean that some indivuduals may be born with stronger or weaker interactive drives (aggressive, sexual, social, for example) than others, including those in their own family. There is also the genetic variation within the structure of the ego itself. An individual may have a comparatively limited capacity to inhibit or modify his interactive energies. Also the ego, in order to do its work properly, must be able to perceive, and there is genetic variation among egos which results in varying capacities to perceive interactive events of any kind.

Concept of Linearity (re: omnipotence)

In watching certain structures in the process of doing therapy I have come to believe that some interactive energies, when stripped of their interface of ego processes, seem to move in a linear or limitless direction. I am reminded of the enormous power of the nuclear explosions that occur when the coherent structure of the atom is destroyed. The analogy is striking for couldn't it be said that nuclear explosions occur when the ego interface of the atom's structure is destroyed? To follow the analogy a step further, stable interactions occur when interactive energy and its ego interface are intact, and unstable energy dispositions occur when the balance between the interface and the interactive energy within is destroyed. However, some nuclear explosions can be harnessed and made productive. Is it possible, then, to harness and direct for productive ends the psychic energies by loosening some ego controls for limited times, or perhaps to overimpose ego controls for opposite reasons at other times? It is conceivable that this is an accurate description of what sometimes occurs in a structure. Those individuals who have constricting egos are helped to loosen them somewhat within the control of a structure, and those who are apparently unable to regulate their interactive energy can be helped to reapply ego controls. Let me continue with another analogy for linearity. With our emphasis on ecology at the present time I am reminded of the fantastic multiplication of rabbits in Australia when they were introduced to that continent. If I remember correctly there were no natural enemies of that species and soon they seemed to be overrunning the entire countryside. That event seems to describe what I mean by the linearity of interactive energy without its ego interface. The energy keeps moving on a straight line towards infinity until it meets up with some kind of limit-setting controls. Those rabbits would have reproduced forever until the natural limits of food and space imposed their effect. The ego has evolutionary values, for its interface seems to direct the interactive energy to more balanced interactions and choices resulting in more mutual satisfactions and more developing complexity and structure in the universe rather than to linear destructiveness and selfishness. That is an interesting concept that is arising. It would seem as if the ego interface recognizes others like itself or at the least recognizes and is able to relate to others whereas without it there would seem to be selfishness and destruction. Ego processes then would lend toward community and mutual growth, whereas ego-less processes would tend to move towards that negative entropic state where all things eventually run down.

To sum up, there seems to be interactive pressure experienced by the individual that would seem to be capable of moving in the direction of infinity were it not for the intervention of outside limiting forces. These forces are then internalized by the ego and used to control the interactive energy.

Consider the little child who is just beginning to feel the sense of his own power. He turns to his mother and says, "I can do anything, I can beat up anybody in the whole world, I can make anybody do what I want them to do. Everybody has to listen to me." Of course a certain amount of this muscle flexing is important for the proper release of his energy store. But it is important that he also be allowed to experience the limits of his energy in situations that would allow him to test his actual powers. Too much of a squelch and he will withdraw from even touching those energies that proved so disastrous to his self-esteem, too little and he will have an inflated sense of his limits and boundaries.

If our boasting little child above were unfortunate enough to have his father die in an accident when the child was developing his aggressive and sexual drives, a number of things might happen to him psychically. Since that little boy would not yet have gained any way of measuring what he actually could or could not do in a reality sense, it would not necessarily seem impossible to him that he did not somehow kill his father. Remember that a child of the age that could speak and say what that little boy was saying could already handle the world of symbol and symbol manipulation quite well. When he was boasting, it would not be terribly unlikely that he was also capable of imagining precisely the conditions under which he would be ruling the world. No doubt, if asked he could describe what he would do, what he would look like, what he would have others do, etc. All those things could seem as real to him as if they were actually occurring. (Remember that humans do have the capacity to treat symbols as if they were real.) Now to the extent that he believed that he actually did kill his father he would be suffering from an "ego break" which would have many implications. One of the functions of the ego is to measure one's own energy potential and to measure the energy potentials of external events. To the extent that one assesses one's energy as infinite, one's ego is no longer fashioned by concrete reality interactions but by fantasized events. I use the following design to demonstrate this.

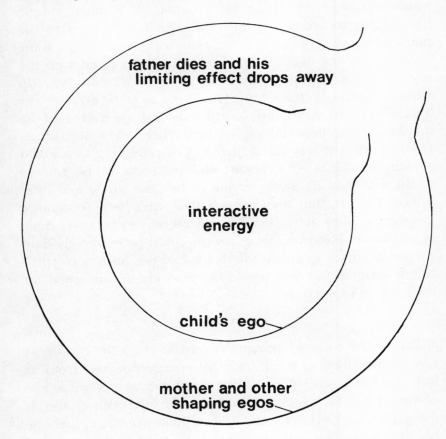

The child can now assume that he has the power to destroy anyone in the entire world and he may take two different pathways to realize this power. He may ascribe to his fantasy and imagination infinite powers and live in a psychotic world of his own, or he may grow up seeking in concrete reality just those powers of control and destruction that he imagined he had. The second would at least keep him sane, if not far more dangerous, and would demonstrate that he knew the difference between fantasy and reality and that he was attempting to place under his ego control those energies which in fantasy he had at his disposal. He would continue his attempt to accrue all the power he could—even to the point of trying to rule the world—until he came across some concrete limiting agency. The average person faced with the circumstances surrounding the little boy does not grow up attempting to rule the world. However, all of us do have the innate capacity to attempt world rule but are restricted by the limitations imposed on us by reality. Most individuals seem to take the less taxing pathway of retreating to a world of fantasy. Those individuals who do seem to go toward world rule may simply be trying to become whole and integrated. That is, they wish to have their egos become as large in reality as they are in fantasy and thereby to become whole in one sense. However, these people could be extremely dangerous, for their aggressive drives would not have been sufficiently capped and they would be relatively unconcerned for the feelings or needs of others.

Part of the surge of power that results from the ego break can be described as the interactive energy released from its hold by the death of the father and the as yet weak ego of the child. This aggressiveness can be understood also as the search for strength and power that would compensate for the protection loss that the child experiences with the loss of the father, who had provided him with security, protection and warmth, as well as limitation for his aggressive energies. With his father gone he must "become his own father." This demands a build-up of strength on either the fantasy or the reality level. If he finds those strengths within himself and not in some surrogate figure in the real world he will cease directing his interactive energy toward the outside world and direct it towards himself, making of himself his own pole-star figure as well as his own interactive target. This can isolate him from relating while making him very strong in certain rigid ways. It can also give him identity problems.

If the child is frightened by the intense surge of energy he experiences at the death of his father, he may experience the shock of the ego break as "I can't handle myself; I am going out of control." This feeling of going out of control could be compounded by a sense of disorientation at the loss of his pole-starfigure father. If his ego collapses from the onslaught of his internal energies, then he may also be incapable of controlling or deflecting the external energies directed at him. That is, his limited capacity for protecting himself, or controlling energy input, may also collapse with the loss of the protection of his father. He may experience the world as rushing in on him like a tidal wave, overwhelming him with stimuli and energy which he cannot handle. It is possible that while one form of his interactive energy is surging out producing an ego break, the world is bursting in through that break. It could be seen that the very coherence of the self of the child would be put to the test just as the cell would be put to the test if its outer membrane were ruptured.

There could be factors other than the death of his father which contribute to a child's emotional disturbance. He might have deficient genetic material, his father may have been insufficient as a limiting, protecting, or orienting figure, or there may be deficiencies in surrogate figures who might have made up for the absence of the father.

Now the "healthy" child who tried to realize the power potential evoked by the death of his father can be diagrammed as below.

child's ego
remains intact

The obvious phallic symbolism of the diagram was relatively unconscious but includes the idea that such a child would also experience the amplification of his sexual energies without the limiting effect of his father. The important fact to consider is that the ego remains intact in this diagram, albeit somewhat enlarged. However, if the child does indeed test his interactive powers in reality and learn to apply his energies toward the common good, such amplification on one's life forces can be used for good effect.

The diagram below for the child who was frightened by the surge of his own aggressive energies, experienced a consequent ego break because he could not handle those energies, and who was unable to control the energies bursting in from the outside due to the disappearance of his father as a protecting figure would demonstrate both omnipotent fantasies and impotent sensations.

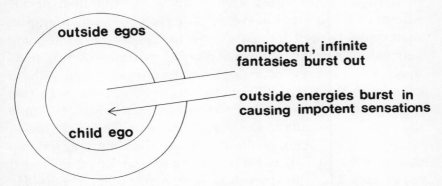

The child's sense of his ego boundaries becomes broken, and he is unable to differentiate himself from either everything, "I am everything, I am the world," or from nothing, "I am nothing, I don't exist." The child's ideation and fantasies would very likely show symbolically his concern with his seemingly enormous powers and the enormous powers of the outside world breaking in. Some of these feelings are reconstructed by the adult client in a structure and they can lead him to wish for a more protected time, perhaps when he was an infant or a foetus within the womb. In this structure he can gain a definite sense of his boundaries which gives him a feeling of security on which to build. Returning to the womb could also have implications such as dying or merging with the universal, and it is important to understand the wishes of the client doing the structure to make certain that he is not using his fantasy to reinforce self-destructive drives.

I must point out the complexity of each event and each choice that is made in a structure. Everything that is done is done by the request or the permission of the client. Nothing is forced on him; he is always in control of his own structure and what goes on in it unless he moves in a very obvious self-destructive way or moves in such a way as to endanger anyone else in the group. At such times the leader or therapist must assess what is going on and then decide whether or not to intervene. The psychomotor therapist, then, must be well trained as well as a sensitive, responding and caring person. Someone reading portions of this book might see the sense of a single interaction and then without examining the complexity of the event or circumstance that he and someone else find themselves in attempt to apply that single description to their interaction. Obviously this is not to be done. Also, obviously, all the deciding and judging that a therapist makes has to be rapid and based on much experience with the client and with many other clients. He cannot stop the therapeutic process for long periods of time while he ponders the implication of the last thing that was done in a structure.

There is a particular structure or structure device which can be valuable for those clients who feel that they are being overwhelmed either by their feelings or by the other members of the group. The structure utilizes symbolic limits and the ideas of "play" and "magic." A circle is drawn around the client and an invisible shield raised from it to surround the client from all sides and from above. I sometimes set up this structure in a pretended playful mood and include the idea of using magic to protect the individual. This structure is not done in lieu of the parental support structure but follows it so that the symbolic extensions of the protection have been preceded by the concrete motoric experience of the protecting parents. The protective shield can be understood as an externalization of the parents' own protective ego processes which can be seen to screen, deflect, modify and inhibit external stimuli directed at the client. When the circle has been made and the screen erected, the client can be told that it is a magic screen that represents his ego and that it can prevent people and feelings from bursting in. Of course this is not done with psychotic patients, or at least not at a time when psychotic patients cannot differentiate between magic and reality, and play and reality. It is more often done with neurotic or normal clients, and the reactions to it are interesting and striking.

The client may or may not assist in the erection of the screen depending on where he is or what he is feeling. Sometimes the outline of the screen can be made concrete by lining pillows along the circumference of the circle. Again, this structure focuses on the client's capacity to control the energy input from the environment.

As an illustration I would like to describe the first time that I used this device of the screen. Let the reader recognize that since there was not a tape recorder running at the time, nor a movie camera, nor did I make special efforts to record this not knowing I would ever want to refer to it, this description is based on my memory of it alone. At some future time I would like to be able to present to professional audiences an actual filming or videotaping of a structure so that the total interaction with all its elements and complexities can be captured and analyzed.

This particular client was female, a professional actress and dancer, attractive, in her late twenties or early thirties, and unmarried, she had attended several weekend workshops previous to this time, so I had some understanding of the central issues that were concerning her and making it difficult for her to perform successfully and to be as comfortable as she wished socially. When it was her turn to do a structure, it was fairly late in the course of the workshop and she stood up saying in effect that it was really necessary for her to "go" now because all the previous structures of the day had "gotten" to her and she felt all pulled apart and vulnerable.

She had her arms wrapped around her body, was holding herself tightly and was slightly stooped over. She opened her eyes only intermittently, and she mentioned that she found it difficult to open them, particularly standing as she was now in front of the entire group. She said she felt like hiding or making people stop looking at her or becoming invisible. She said she was feeling some panic and a great deal of anxiety. As I recall this particular case, there were some clues which indicated to me that the first step should be a control step rather than an expression step. In previous structures she had shown a tendency to symbiotically blend with her positive figures and to move in a direction toward fusion rather than clarification of feelings and figures. That is, the usual objectivity that I find necessary for a client to maintain in a structure was not always apparent in her case. My analogy for a client in a structure is that of a deep-sea diver. The client has got to have sufficient ego awareness "manning the pumps on the surface," so to speak, while he makes the deep-sea dive to explore his unexpressed interpersonal interactive energy. If there is no one on the surface manning the pumps then the client is not in a good position to do a structure for there is no one "watching and knowing and learning" to gain all the value of the structure, and the structure is something that he lets happen to him rather than something that he is "doing". The client is then giving up too much of his autonomy and is indicating a willingness to move toward dependency and passivity.

When I perceive in a client this ego deficiency, I request that he do an exercise in conscious voluntary movement, which tests the capacity for controlling the body while "turning off" the emotions. This is not to say that I have a tendency to move away from strong emotions and their expression in a structure, for that is the energy of a structure and without strong emotions being used and clarified there would be little growth and change as a result. However, there are situations when the goal of the client apparently is not so much to learn and know and grow from the experience but more to swim in the primitive experience without learning to glean anything from it, a kind of move toward omnipotent emotionality. This exercise measures ego controls and willingness and capacity to modify interpersonal interactive energy. Some clients, when they attempt this exercise, report tremendous conflict in the form of an inner dialogue. One voice says "You'll never get me to do it," and the other "I will too, you'll do what I say."

To return to the description of the structure, the client had had some very successful experiences with the protective and nurturing positive mother and father figures in previous structures, and the way she was holding herself seemed to indicate that she needed either to hold or be held and that the structure should be directed toward filling this need. She seemed to me to be able at this point to use the type of structure based on the concept of the ego as skin. Her body posture indicated to me her need for this protective envelope of a membrane. Either she could have gone to the parents and they could have embraced or she could have attempted to do the protecting herself. I gave her the choice after describing to her the structure I had in mind. She agreed to explore the circle and shield. The circle was set up and the shield described and its powers to inhibit penetration outlined.

She said, "Now what?" I said, "Now test it, see if it works. Have people move toward the shield and see if it stops them. Group members were directed by her to come toward the circle and then were to be "bounced off" by the invisible shield. As each individual group member did so, she became excited by seeing them unable to get beyond the shield and she grew delighted and wanted to test it again and again, she had every member of the group including myself walk toward her and then bounce off when he hit the shield. She began to look and behave in a more relaxed manner. She stood straighter and did not hold herself any longer. She had on dark glasses and was able to take them off once she experienced the effectiveness of her shield. This indicated that she now could open her eyes without feeling as if the world were coming in on her. In reference to this it should be noted that both her mother and her father had too soon placed her in a position of responsibility for the younger members of the family. She was expected to help care for and rear them much too soon and experienced very little of her mother or her father as protective or supporting figures. Both parents in some measure had turned toward her for support. More importantly, both parents made it clear to her from a very early age that they, individually (they related to her not as parents together for they had a poor relationship with one another, but individually, as peers and fantasy lovers), found her very attractive sexually—which she was. Thus when she felt the world coming in on her, she felt the threat of sexual invasion, followed by sexual guilt, and beneath that a profound nurturant deficit which found expression in conscious and unconscious wishes for symbiotic union. You can see the number of different directions a structure could have taken. It could have followed the direction of the interactive energy and clarified the need, organ of expression and target and unfused the differences between oral nurturance and sexual relations, etc. I point this out to indicate that there is no one single way to work in a structure and that individual therapists might take entirely different areas to emphasize and to work with or the client might just as effectively see what was going on and choose one area to work with over another.

Now that she could open her eyes, the world no longer rushed into her through her eyes. Here the ego was represented by the very skin of the eyelids. If they were closed the stimulus was turned off. Now she could open her eyes and still hold off invasion because she had internalized control of the magic shield. Perhaps she could also open her eyes because she no longer was experiencing the shame and guilt of the sexual aspect of the invasion. She may have been guilty for her own wishes to take the world in sexually. (In subsequent workshops we dealt with her sexual omnipotence.)

The experience of seeing the people bounce off the shield at first delighted her and then puzzled her. Was it fair or all right for her to bounce people off when they wanted to come to her? The crucial question of the rights of the individual! As I recall, either we set up good parents or I voiced the opinion of the good parents that she had the right to keep people out of her ego or her life if she wanted to, that nobody had the right to come in on her when she didn't want it, that no matter how much anyone "needed" her in any way that did not give him the license to invade. This made her cry for it reminded her of specific events when she was psychologically and perhaps literally invaded (by a recent lover), she got very angry. We dealt with that anger by having an accommodator role play the negative contemporary, that is the negative aspects of her lover and begin to move at her in an invading way. The client found herself unable to fight him off and began to collapse. Before she collapsed completely, however, we had the good parents fight off the invader. The client then wanted to be held by the good parents, and it was decided that they would hold her without piercing or entering her circle. They reached in with her permission and put their arms around her. After she was comforted for a period, she wanted to test her own ability to control the approach of the group. This time she wanted to see if she could direct the individual group members toward her and stop them by a command or a gesture rather than depend on the shield to bounce them off. She practiced this for a while with individual group members but it was pointed out to her that she almost permitted each person to cross the line of the circle before stopping him. This she now understood as a wish on her part to be invaded which she demonstrated in the guise of testing the control she had over when to stop the invader. This was good learning for it pointed out very graphically to her that even when she was in complete control she tended to invite or risk invasion.

Now she wondered if perhaps she let some people get closer because she wanted really to be close to some people. This reminded her of her negative contemporary who had been fought off by the parents, and she now wanted to see if she alone could defend herself against him. She thought for a moment as she conjured up the memory of the event and then with some fear directed the group member who was playing the negative contemporary to come after her and to repeat plaintively that he needed her. She at first hesitated and then pushed him away. Then, when she directed him to be more forceful, she successfully directed more anger at him without being overwhelmed by her feelings or by his proximity. She then wished to be close to a positive contemporary figure. The group member playing this role moved toward her as she indicated, and she instructed him to stand on the outside of her circle and hug her while she stood on the inside of the circle. She held him for a period of time in a loving embrace and then said that she wished to feel the experience of being in her circle.

She decided to move about in her circle, and she moved in a comfortable and somewhat sensual way saying that she felt "inside" her body. When asked what she meant by that, she said that she did not know how to explain it except that it was a new and pleasant sensation and that she felt comfortable being in her body and that she did exist in her body and that she could feel it and that it felt good. Perhaps I pointed it out to her, or perhaps she began speaking about it or feeling it herself, but she began to move her hands over the skin of her face and her body and feel as if she were within her skin and that it was her boundary. The client began to speak in a tone of wonder and pleasure about her feeling that she was inside her body and that she ended where her skin ended and that nobody could get into her or at her or overwhelm her if she didn't need it or want to invite or permit it. The world seemed a safer place to her, the sounds of the world were not hostile, invading sounds, and the sight of people was not embarassing, or invading, but pleasant. She felt that she was a distinct person and saw others as distinct people. She felt the structure was over and wanted to leave the circle. The problem then was what to do with the circle. When she stepped out of it, was she going to walk away from her ego? She decided to place the pillows one at a time against her body and then to put them to one side not in a circular order. Each pillow individually was touched to a different part of her body, and by this "magical" act she took on the powers or the qualities of the pillows, and the pillows were permitted to become just pillows again and placed against walls and on chairs.

"Magic," if handled properly, has seemed to me to be a useful tool in a structure. Of course I do not mean magic in the usual sense but more in the sense of investing a symbol with magical powers and then internalizing those powers or using them in some concrete graphic way.

The result of the structure was that she found energies or systems of thinking within herself and systems of behavior within herself which she could use toward controlling the energy input of the world.

In subsequent workshops this client indicated, both by her behavior and by her words, that a real change had occurred in her as a result of that particular structure which, of course, had been led up to by previous structures. She reported that she was working more in the theatre and

performing with greater ease, that her interpersonal relationships were less overwhelming and that she had more control
of her feelings of panic and anxiety.

Thus in my view one of the important results of her structure was that she became able to handle the world through
her own efforts. Of course, earlier structures had helped
to bring her to that point. It is also true that there will un-
doubtedly be future structures in which she may need to
rely temporarily on the good parents, but that is done only
to give the "child aspect," or memories of one's self, the
opportunity to experience what it might have been like to
have these good parents and then to assist the "child" to
grow and do for himself what was being done for him.

Dealing with the Spill from the Ego Break

Whenever there is an ego break, there always follow the
problems of omnipotence and impotence, plus the releasing
of the interpersonal interactive energy into other systems.

Thus in the event of an ego break the problem of limitations must be handled. I have found that those clients who
have lived successfully through an interactive event that permitted the release of excess aggressive or sexual energies—for
instance, where there have been deaths in the family or symbolic unconscious seductions in the family that led to fantasies
of aggressive or sexual omnipotence—have not become psychotic but do have a somewhat unrealistic assessment of their
powers. Those individuals usually have come to enjoy their
sense of added power, and when the time comes to limit
them in a structure, there can be quite a conflict. This is a very
complex problem and I should take some time to outline
the various aspects of it. On the one hand those individuals
might show some pride in and even depend somewhat for
their identity on assessments of their own power. On the
other hand they might be extremely guilty or ashamed of
their assumed power and find a lot of discomfort in the use

of it or the contemplation of it. Some may find it impossible to use their power in any realistic way in the world and others may find it impossible even to think of using those energies without experiencing anxiety or guilt. Some may express or acknowledge the sense of omnipotence only in some indirect or symbolic or unconscious way. However the omnipotence is experienced, when the structure moves toward limiting that power, even those clients who began the structure choosing to be limited in either their sexual or aggressive energies find they have a tremendous drive to express and realize their omnipotence in a motoric, direct emotional way.

Let us take a more specific example, that of a young man training to be a psychotherapist, a person with a high level of conscious understanding and awareness of himself. He was married, although the marriage was not considered by either him or his wife to be at all successful and was well on its way toward dissolution. His relationship with his mother involved her excessive preoccupation with his marital satisfactions, implying specifically his sexual satisfactions. Mother was fairly seductive to him when he was a child. She dressed in front of him, asked for his assistance on snaps and bra straps, and gave him baths until he was ten years old or older. On both the conscious and unconscious levels, the client felt that his mother was entirely available to him sexually, and his fantasies always included her in bed with him. Father was, paradoxically, the more passive parent, even though the mother's appearance and behavior were femininely passive. The client wanted the father to be more aggressive and obviously capable of relating to the mother in a sexually satisfying way. There was nothing this client wanted more than to be free of his fantasy relationship and his real relationship with his mother, both of which interfered far too much in his life on all levels. Yet when the good parents in the structure stood in front of him in an embrace and said that they loved only each other sexually and that neither would direct any sexual behavior to him, he smirked and said to the mother, "I can have you anytime I want you." His attempts to separate the mother from the father were intense on both a physical and a mental base. That is, he attempted to figure out ways to overcome the obstacle of a mattress folded in half that was placed in front of him as a buffer between himself and his parents, a usual practice for this type of structure. He tried, for example, to climb over the mattress, to break it apart, to break through it, and to go around the ends, as well as many other imaginative and cunning solutions to gain access to the mother. He worked at it as if his life depended on it but was relieved when he could not succeed. However, the structure was not over. When he was offered his positive contemporary figure to be his own lover, he was obviously disinterested in her. I suggested that he turn back to his interest in his negative mother (in order to utilize the sexual interactive energy that was not moving toward his contemporary), who was now separated from the negative father. I directed her to behave seductively toward the son as he had described his real mother doing, and he readily went to her. Parenthetically, I was actually hoping or expecting him to limit his own responses to his seductive mother for this is what occurs in the majority of cases when such fantasies are permitted to be played out. The client usually makes one or two steps toward the parent offering herself sexually and then retreats. This is not what happened at this time. He gladly moved into her open-armed embrace and looked at me and said, "Should I go on?" I fully expected him to retreat at any moment and said, "Sure, go ahead." He embraced her and then said, "I feel like lying down with her." Once again I reassured him that it was all right to go ahead since I was sure he would pull back at any moment. He continued however until he was half-lying on her with one leg over her. At that point I realized he was not going to stop his action, and to test my conclusion I suggested that he lie on top of the mother with his legs between her separated legs. This he did readily and then made no move to pull away. I waited perhaps ten seconds and then intervened and said, "As both the group leader and as good father I cannot let you fuck your mother. Get off." Now he was ready to do battle on another level, and demanded, "What's wrong with having your mother sexually anyway?" Now the encounter was with myself as group leader and with him as himself. We were no longer playing our roles within the structure, but he still had to be limited. I was adamant that he would not have his mother in any group of mine.

I wish to point out that the limiting must be done whether it is on a structure level or on the reality level, whether it is on a behavior level or on an ideational level. The client was vehement in arguing for the custom of incest on a philosophical level and saw nothing intrinsically wrong with it. He ignored for the moment the obvious havoc that the realistic possibility of his sleeping with his mother was playing with his marital life. His strong belief in his omnipotence was demonstrated by his tenacity in holding to the ideas and fantasies of sleeping with his mother which included his philosophical argument for incest. The client fought for the mother both on the physical and on the ideational level and said, "What do you mean I can't have her. I had her all my life. She's mine and always will be."

A client may experience separation from the target of his omnipotence as being separated from his life. He will not give up this target easily, yet it is most important that he does. Limiting the child in reality at the age of four, or whenever his aggressive and sexual energies are at the stage which is ripe for clarification, exercise and limits, is relatively simple compared to attempting that limitation years later after a lifetime of habit of feeling and behaving as they have grown accustomed to. It takes a strong leader to impose those limits both in the role playing aspects and in reality, for clients will not hesitate to attack the leader on an emotional and personal level when they are being restricted by him. Even the client may very much want those limits imposed, at the same time he will fight desperately to maintain the past pattern of feeling and behaving. If the limitation is successful and the client accepts the limits on the physical and ideational level, then the leader has to face the consequences of that loss of omnipotence and loss of target, however misplaced.

In the case I am describing, I spoke to the client in the combined role of therapist and good father, telling him in effect that no matter how many times he may have felt he could "get" his mother in the past I simply would not allow him to do that any longer with this mother, and I indicated the negative mother in the structure. I expressed anger at the negative mother for having been seductive and "threw her away" to model for the client the anger that should have been directed at the mother for behaving in such a way that contributed to marital and sexual difficulties. "But I want her," the client said. "I'm sorry but you can never have her," I replied. The client then began to feel grief at the loss and began to cry. The good parents held him while he cried and the good father emphasized his strength and assured the client that he would always be there. After he stopped crying, the client felt some need to be nurtured by the good mother, and that was done. He then wanted to see the good parents together and demanded that there be no space between them. If there was any space separating them, he attempted to widen the rift physically but was prevented from succeeding. Then he wished to return to his positive contemporary, and this time he embraced her with a great deal more interest and motivation. Still, he was not done and found that he was growing angry at his negative mother. He expressed his anger to his mother and that changed his level of relationship once again with his contemporary. While

he was with her, he commented that he found himself thinking of his mother and that the two figures seemed somewhat
merged in his mind. I suggested that the two figures stand
one behind the other and that he consciously attempt to separate them. The client noted that it sent shivers up his spine
to see the two of them like that and said that it was just
the way it was in his mind. I said, "Sort them out. Pull them
apart and away from each other." This he did and then
pushed the negative mother far away from him and said,
"Go away and don't interfere in my life." Then he returned
to his contemporary figure with more commitment of feeling
than ever. Following an embrace with the contemporary he
felt that the structure was over.

I can report on the followup with this client. He commented that his relationship with his wife had improved and
that his work had improved in important ways. He was in
therapy on a one-to-one- basis and in these sessions had developed new perspectives on some of the feelings brought out
in the structure: He had discovered also many new feelings
and patterns of behavior that had not appeared before which
gave him a different understanding of the energy distributions within himself. Previous to this structure he had not
been able to express openly many of the feelings that came
out during the structure. In terms of this chapter his structure highlights the emotional investment in omnipotent feelings even if these feelings are not at all acted on or experienced fully in reality. The structure formation permits the
feelings to come to the surface and then to be clarified,
limited and dealt with. If not dealt with, those feelings remain
in a state of frozen potentiality, for this client commented
that in reality he found it difficult to let loose either with
his aggressive feelings or with his sexual feelings. Yet paradoxically when those sexual feelings were released in the
structure they moved swiftly and inexorably toward the
mother and there was great investment in their fulfillment

and great pain in their limiting. Again, paradoxically, following the limitation those energies were more available on a reality level than they had been previously.

Other clients might have responded differently than the one described even had they had similar histories. It is possible that another person might become compulsively interested in having sexual experiences with older women without feeling any satisfaction or pleasure. Others might do the same with pleasure but without the ability of having relations with women of their own generation, making it impossible for them to marry and have a family of their own.

Without going into any further detail it should be clear to the reader that this type of formulation permits a frame of reference within which certain moves can be made with a sense of direction and purpose. That is, the formulation that the ego is similar to the skin of the self with feelings and energies flowing in or out, permits plans of action for therapeutic interventions and structures that clarify complex emotional relationships and behavioral patterns.

To sum up, the ego appears to be those processes within an individual which permit awareness of one's shape and energy distribution and potential and awareness of the energy distributions and potential of the outside world. In other words the ego processes include that of perception both within and without, with concomitant access to energy and motor systems that can modify the direction of interpersonal interactive energy. So with all the interactive energy and motor systems we must include the ego processes which perceive, oversee, modulate, modify and perhaps inhibit those interactions. If the ego controls are partially dislocated or stripped away, the released energies burst into the direction of infinity and omnipotence. The ego which is stretched to shapelessness by the onslaught might identify itself with the universe rather than with finite individual figures. The energies that are loosed are rarely available on the reality level but seem shunted to the bodiless inner screen of fantasies and dreams. This particular shunting action includes the emotional phenomena of guilt, shame, self-punishment, suicidal feelings, and the depletion of energy. In the next chapter I will explore those phenomena under the heading of the superego or the species ego.

CHAPTER 7

The superego, to use the Freudian term, is in my understanding a system for catching the interactive energies that slip past the ego and would seem to endanger the species. That is, in some respects the system works for the safety and satisfaction of others rather than for the safety and satisfaction of the self. Therefore I prefer the term "species ego" since the system functions as a safety valve for the species.

In a rough analogy the species ego can be seen as a massive circuit breaker for the emotional system, as a huge magnetic deflector which directs the aggressive energies toward the self for self-punishment or even self-destruction, or as a shunter of interactive energy from one energy system to another. A visual representation of the deflector could be the curving of a barrel of a gun so that the open end of the barrel faces the gunner. The idea of punishment is included in this system as well as the idea of loss of supportive figures as a result of certain behavior.

Some people are born with a greatly developed sense of "the other" and some with a deficient sense of "the other." The function of the ego is related to the satisfactions of the self through the gaining of appropriate matchings between interactive energy and target. Sometimes the species ego seems to coerce the ego for its own purposes. To put it another way, an individual may stop himself from performing a certain act that would be harmful to others because he fears the disapproval of supportive figures.

By and large the species ego is a more primitive apparatus than the ego. Perhaps a simile might be that when the normal ego interactive energy systems develop balances that do not endanger the species, the superego remains unused until there is an energy overload that would burn out the system. This, then, would seem to indicate that the species ego system includes self-preservation as well as preservation of the species. For example, when an ego break occurs and the interactive energy can move toward infinity, there seems to be an instant shunting of the interactive energy over to the symbolic system, the dream or fantasy system, or even to the perception system (hallucinations). This shunting prevents the total system from being "burned out" by a cataclysmic burst of energy on the interpersonal interactive level, such as a catatonic excitement.

When the species ego functions as a circuit breaker, it turns off the energy in an interpersonal interactive system. The ego can use the voluntary motor system to modify or modulate behavior to achieve greater congruence with the real world and therefore greater satisfaction for the interactive processes. The species ego modifies behavior not to increase satisfaction as the ego does, but to thwart or punish the self to stop the action. The species ego, then, is a last resort, or stop-gap measure, in the event that all other things fail.

This perhaps explains the use of the species ego when, for example, a father's limiting powers are subverted by the aggressive and sexual interpersonal interactive energies of his son and he calls upon the forces of society or God to stop the son in his transgressions. The father may say, "I can't stop you but you will burn in hell for what you have done. God will punish you for this." The father is attempting to arouse the species ego processes in the son, whom he has limited capacity to control through his own interactions. Parents, then, can use the species ego constraints when their own ego interactions fail to do the job of limiting. The device is available as an innate possibility, and it can be overused to modify behavior.

The concept of taboo falls very nicely into this construct. When the individual behaves in a manner that is beyond the strictures of the community, the species ego processes take over and the individual may die. He may *die* by his own hand or he may die *because his very life energies are "turned off"* just as the circuit breaker turns off the current. Thus, in some cases more than the forbidden interactive behavior is turned off. By this I mean that some individuals may die in certain cultures when they have transgressed. They do not feel simply a loss of aggressive or sexual energy but experience the life drain on the metabolic, vegetative level.

The species ego must have perception mechanisms connected with it, for it must be able to measure energy output (just as a fuse essentially measures energy output) in order to function. Under poor genetic or interpersonal circumstances a species ego "fuse" could be set at a low voltage and might shunt energy at very little provocation. Individuals with such a sensitive species ego would tend to be very cautious and timid and be exceedingly careful not to do anything that might cause anyone the slightest pain or disturbance. Their energy output would be low, and they would tend to be very compliant. In a schizophrenic case of this nature, the interactive energy would be omnipotent fantasies and hallucinations. The normal timid individual would still have his interactive energies largely available to him in their ordinary capacities although quite reduced in voltage.

In the same case of poor genetic and interpersonal conditions a species ego fuse could, on the other hand, be set too high, and this individual would see barely anything from the other person's view and would have very little control over his aggressive or sexual impulses. This is a classic example of character disorder. The limiting of this individual would have to be strict to develop the stunted species ego faculties. Perhaps he could have his own interpersonal needs become dependent on the satisfaction of others' needs so that he might develop a species ego out of his own self-interest. This situation raises the necessity for inner monitoring or perception of one's energies, which brings out two issues: the species ego processes must borrow perception of outer and inner events from ego processes; and that the self-perception must function to censor or monitor the direction and flow of the energy before it becomes action.

In the process of treating the character disorder individual, the limiting figures should be with him as much as possible to watch and monitor his energy flow, for if he is alone he can say to himself, "No one can see what I am doing so it doesn't matter what I get away with. No one will ever be the wiser." The normal individual can act in a situation as if he were being watched by others and that tends to limit his action. Having a species ego is like having an all-seeing monitor constantly within one's self. It is as if a piece of ourselves or our egos did not individuate and remained universal, omnipotent, and omniscient and we named it God or our conscience. At the outset of this book I speculated regarding life and interactive energy that all life in some inexplicable way knew all other life, that everything was related to everything else, and that interactive energy "knew" its target because the target "matched" the energy. I also speculated that human life moved through the process of individuating from the universal and that therefore living partook in some fashion of the universal. The universal stance would seem to me to include the statement "I am you and you are me and we are all one together." The species ego processes seem to imply the use of that concept in the use of the Golden Rule, which says, "Do unto others as you would have others do unto you," which could mean that you and others are essentially the same.

This paradox of being at one time universal and individual seems connected to what I understand as species ego. Species ego learning or developing seems to have to include one's view of the world as well as what one identifies one's self with. If I see myself as the same as all animals, I would find it difficult to treat animals any differently than I treat myself and would find it impossible to eat them. Vegetarians behave in just that way. Other individuals who take a broader view of identification with nature find it difficult to kill or consume anything but the bare necessities of life. Other individuals who would suffer tremendous pangs of conscience and guilt if they injured a human being can butcher animals without the slightest hesitation for they do not identify with them. All wars include massacres of people by troops who are described as perfectly loving men to their own kinfolk. When the enemy is seen as not like one's self, or not quite human, one does not have to control one's behavior toward them. Obviously, then, species ego processes are vitally connected with learning. The capacity to convert or shunt one's energies to other systems, to direct one's energies to one's self, to turn off one's energies are innate and somehow built into the human psychic system. But the events and situations which trigger those responses are learned and developed within certain frames of reference. The qualities of the species ego which seem to be found in all cultures and which seem to be somewhat unlearned are the qualities of identification with the target of one's energies, that is, "He is I," and the quality of internal observation which is likened to being observed by God or by some authority figure. In other words the species ego possibilities are there in the human psyche but the names and situations are learned in each culture.

The species ego, then, gains its energies from the ego and, by splitting off a portion of the ego to serve as universal and god-like forces, exercises control of the self in the name of those forces. Thus, when the interactive energies become too great for ego control and one begins to feel omnipotent, the superego, in the name of God and omniscience, redirects those energies back to the self! With the shunting of the energy into the realm of fantasy, hallucination and delusion, as it is in the case of psychotics, the ego just about disappears with the enhancement of the omnipotent aspects of one's self. All or almost all of one's self becomes identified with the universal, the omniscient and the omnipotent. Psychosis in this frame of reference is the result of the superego's exercising too much control which causes the imbalance of the total self and the loss of the ego. The individual, then, loses his identity in the usual process of individuation, and those aspects of the ego that have been split off to create the supergo in the name of the universal become dominant. Because the psychotic never tests his beliefs about himself in the world of motoric concrete reality and because his energy is shunted away from the body and into fantasy, hallucination and delusion via manipulation of the symbolic perceptual world, he never realizes the fallacy of his view of himself. If, then, there is not sufficient parenting at an early age to emphasize the ego and individuation in the motoric, concrete reality base, the individual can develop a sick species ego by doing for himself on the symbolic level what should have been done for him on the concrete level. The untested symbolic level, not based on reality interactions and not ego-oriented but universal-omnipotent-oriented (since it has transcended the parental figures and done symbolically what they have not done concretely), identifies more of the self with that split-off portion of the ego devoted to self-scrutiny for the purpose of identification with the universal, that is, the species ego. It strikes me that most pathology seems to move in the direction of permitting the symbolic to dominate the actual or concrete. It also permits species ego processes to dominate ego processes. It stops the process of interaction with people and moves to manipulation of things and ideas. At the very least pathology creates energy imbalances and arena confusions. By that I mean the confusion between the interactive energy arenas which normally distinguish food, people and things.

The positive applications of species ego processes would seem to be toward the development of ethical relationships with food, people and things. That is, to respect in a healthy way those targets as if they were somewhat like one's self, which indeed in a philosophical if not real sense they are. If the ego can be understood to be a system of energies which assist the organism in the process of maintaining its wholeness and integrity, the species ego can be understood as a process which assists the species in maintaining its wholeness and integrity. So that given a choice between the individual and the species, the species ego sees to it that the species wins out even at the price of death to the individual.

Punishment

One regularly sees in psychomotor structures angry actions arising in an individual which the individual then either suppresses or directs toward himself. The good parent figures usually speak to that inner-directed anger and tell the client that his anger is all right and that he doesn't have to hurt himself with it. It is not sufficient simply to say that, however, for the client usually will begin to explore why he is bad for having such feelings, which often are related to some event when his anger was the cause of much pain and consternation in the family. In some cases the client may have thrown a rock which nearly killed a playmate and since that time he has had difficulty expressing his anger outwardly. He may consider himself a murderer in actuality and remove himself from many interactions for fear that he might endanger someone's life. He may possibly remain in nominal relations with people but without investing interpersonal interactive energy in those relationships. He may treat himself and others as either things or ideas.

If the client is convinced that he is bad and should be punished, he may become accident prone, so that indeed he does experience pain regularly at his own hands. He may have a low estimate of his capacity to control his feelings and may spend a lot of time telling himself that he is bad and is unworthy of human love and caring. So we have the phenomenon of the angry emotions not only turned off or shunted to another system but directed toward the self in accidential injuries on the physical level or in self-punishing ideas on the emotional or mental level. The self-punishment or request for punishment from the outside (which also is a regular occurrence with guilt-ridden persons) can be utilized as a negative nurturant or relationship input. Therefore, when the species ego directs the energy inward and does not allow its outward expression, this energy has the secondary value of being utilized as a negative nurturance mode. Thus, some clients adamantly hold on to their guilt for they are being nurtured by it and do not expect to receive love or support from any external figures because of their feeling of unworthiness. Obviously, then, when an energy disposition is dealt with, the therapist must look at the dynamic implications of it in terms of its intra-psychic function. That is, the guilt cannot be given up until a replacement mode is available and is desired by the client. Without the replacement the client would be left with a painful deficit in his interpersonal interactive system.

This presents an interesting picture in terms of energy dispositions. An ego is developed as a child experiences the appropriate relationships with his parents which permit the normal growth from universal to individual, from concrete to abstract, from dependent to independent. If the parenting is deficient in some ways, it increases the child's anger and frustration. If the child expresses the anger and the parents cannot handle it, they may tell him he is bad and arouse his guilt. This type of situation will force the child to turn away from his parents as satisfying figures and turn to others if they are available. If others are not available, he will turn to himself too soon and will injure his capacity to receive nurturance and relate in a satisfying way. His anger will reinforce his sense of omnipotence.and ability to transcend his parents and his species ego processes will shunt his angry energy toward himself. Now he receives that energy from himself and may use it in lieu of warmth from his parents, making it harder still for him to turn toward external figures. Everything that happens leads him further away from relationships and more toward directing his energy toward himself and narrowing his exchange of interactive energy with the world. None of this is prescribed or perceived as a healthy or satisfying solution; however, it has its value in that it presents a stable energy condition. Perhaps this is where the issue of resistance can be understood. Naturally the patient is unwilling to disturb the equilibrium of his energy distributions, particularly so if he has not been given any obvious and clearly defined alternative. Psychomotor therapy, because of its emphasis on motoric and nurturant satisfactions, permits an energy alternative that is not available in traditional psychotherapy. We can point out the inappropriateness of the guilt "eating" and indicate that good positive nurturance is available from the good mother. The good parents can also point out that no matter how angry the client gets, they can handle the anger. Thus the client can learn to handle his anger because the good parents permit him to express it in a limiting structure. In this way his angry emotional energy is no longer available to be directed toward himself in a negative nurturant way and his pathological hold on the inward-turned, angry-guilt energy is broken when his anger is expressed in a contained, motoric way.

When the good parents hold the client in the limiting structure, they represent the reinstating of ego controls over the powerful angry emotions that previously had broken through the ego bounds and had been directed back upon the client by his species ego. Once that energy is contained within the ego, it is less available as a source of negative nurturance from the self and the client is in a position to look outside himself for relationship and nurturance. The limiting structure reinstates positive parent figures who are larger and stronger than the client and who can be used by him as external pole-star figures in his identity-orienting process. In short, the limiting structure places the client in a position where he can relate to others again and use his body safely in a motoric, concrete way without the negative intervention of his species ego processes.

Whenever the species ego has swung strongly into action, one can assume that there has been an ego break, that there will be symbolic rather than direct expression of powerful feelings, and that the person will identify more with the universal than with the individual (that is, he will develop feelings of omnipotence and personal grandeur). This person will tend to withdraw from interactions with other people and will prefer to interact with his inner self; he will lose a sense of competent identity with other individuals as there will be no external figures powerful and stable enough to orient from and he therefore will orient from his own omnipotence but without external, concrete motor confirmation of his power. Of course there are many variations of intensity within this type of disturbance, but I think that the characteristics described above are generally true and provide good frames of reference within which to work when clients exhibit the kinds of feelings and ideation that bespeak an ego break.

When there is that ego break, the species ego may interrupt the energies as described above, or there may be great pressure on the ego to grow and actually to realize the powers that exist on the fantasy or symbolic level in order to remain in motoric concrete relationship with reality. Those figures in history who have accumulated vast powers seem to me to fall into the latter category. If they were prevented from accumulating or realizing their powers, they would have to face the consequences of becoming severely emotionally ill for then they would have to revert to symbolic, delusional experiences of that power instead of the real concrete demonstration of it. I postulate that these figures represent a massive struggle to remain sane while attempting to realize the energy releases of their ego breaks. They attempt to stretch their egos over the entire surface of the earth to bring it all under their dominion. If they were to find that they could not demonstrate their power in a real and concrete way, they would face the spectre of insanity or those energies would then turn toward the self in a destructive way.

There is a question whether or not the limiting structure in psychomotor therapy tends to reduce ambition in clients. Experience has not shown this to happen, but the opposite is frequently true—there has been a general raising of competence. It is, after all, the rare individual who does take the path toward world dominion. He must represent a unique combination of abilities as well as circumstances which propel him toward his destiny. The average person faced with an ego break tends to move toward pathology, that is, withdrawal from reality and relationships, and to experience the species ego processes strongly enough to be shunted by them to symbolic delusional expression and experience.

The relative genetic strength of the interactive-energy ego and the species ego would have to be taken into account in these cases and would permit great variation among individuals, for example, the real accumulation of power plus great amounts of guilt and negative nurturance. I do not think that powerful historical figures such as Alexander or Caesar can be called simply psychopaths; surely there may be a reduction of species ego strength in their cases, but psychopaths tend to disorganize society, while these powerful figures exhibit strong needs to organize society as well as to hold dominion over it. Psychopaths seem temporary and puny in comprison to these figures and would seem to have weak egos as well as weak species egos. Consider their inability to contain their interactive energy, to time its release and to match it with the appropriate figures. These historical military leaders had great discipline and impulse control and fit more readily, in this rather general overview, into the description of strong ego and interactive energy with too little limiting from their parents.

I would like to turn now to a specific, recent case which demonstrates some of the factors described above. This client arrived for a weekend workshop, and it was clear to me that sexuality would be an issue for her from the start. She was a psychology intern in her late twenties and had a manner of bearing and dress that aroused sexual fantasies in me at once. Her eyes were "receptive" and "inviting" but there hovered about her a minor air of "dirtiness," sloppiness or messiness that jarred slightly with the sexual attractiveness. As a workshop leader and therapist I have grown accustomed to a certain amount of sexual energy directed toward me, and I have watched the expression of it and my responses to it change as the client changes. I have come to recognize a certain pattern of behavior and my responses to it over a period of years. Some clients have been able to arouse in me a powerful wish to have sexual relations with them. When I saw those patients on a one to one basis, it became difficult to work because of the sexual arousal and the concomitant guilt and anxiety it produced in me. I would find myself having thoughts and feelings that could be verbalized as "I must divorce my wife and marry this person because she is the most attractive and beautiful person I have ever seen."

I felt consternation the first times those powerful feelings and fantasies presented themselves. As time went on, in the course of therapeutic change, those clients began to become less and less sexual objects, more female people, more interesting as people and less frantically desirable as sexual objects. Those changes bespoke my own changes and growth as well as my client's changes and growth. Inevitably those clients had to deal with their own powerful wishes for father figures and their usually unconscious sexual luring of the father figure. These women were attractive sexually not only to me but to men in general and they illustrate the fact that people (not only clients) tend to produce in the environment the kinds of responses to which their personality structures are prepared to relate. Some people on first meeting a person provoke in him the fantasy and wish to beat them, for example, and I have learned to pay attention to those feelings and fantasies that are aroused in me on first encounters with a client and to examine their origins either in me or in the client's behavior and manner. If it is clear to me that the feeling originates largely in the client, I can then begin to make certain assumptions regarding the history of the need to produce that response in others.

In the case of the client in question, I recognized my responses to her attractiveness but without guilt. However, I wondered at the "dirty" little girl messages and held that perception in readiness for use in the structures that would be forthcoming in the weekend. I was already prepared to deal with powerful sexual wishes in her for her father and in anticipation of her demands had formulated some responses.

At the beginning of each weekend workshop, following the slow accumulation of clients in the room and the low-level social interaction that ensues (learning something about the other person much as one does at a cocktail party), there is a more formal process where each person gives his name and occupation and says something about his goals for the workshop and possibly something about reactions to the previous workshop. I then present some outline of the psychomotor process as an aid to orientation to the weekend which in this case included some statement about negative nurturances and primary modes of relationship. I said something about these people I mentioned above who produce wishes in others to hit them, about others who make people wish to humiliate them, others who make people wish to feed them and about those people who provoke sexual fantasies in others. At that point the client under discussion interrupted my talk to interject, "What's wrong with relating sexually?" I clarified that indeed there was nothing wrong with relating sexually but that I was pointing it out as a sometimes primary mode of relationship which excluded other modes of relationship and was out of balance with the total personality. Obviously the client felt the need to defend sexual relating more strongly than did anyone else in the group. At the very least it brought attention to the fact that sexuality and its level of use would be a factor for her.

The next event that told me much more about her occurred in the exercise of the fall-catch. In this exercise the group members individually stand in the relaxed species stance, permit their center of gravity to fall forward beyond their feet and then allow their reflexive responses to move them to catch their balance rather than catching themselves by stepping forward voluntarily. When it was this client's turn, I felt for some reason that I cannot consciously understand that it might be important for her to have some supporting figure right in front of her in case she wished to fall straight down. For the fall-catch is sometimes useful as a suicidal or self-destructive barometer in that those clients who are feeling that way will fall straight down without catching their balance and possibly will injure themselves. Perhaps I thought that this might be the case with this client because of the way she did the stance; at any rate, I was about to speak to her and suggest that good parent figures be placed in front of her. When I started to speak she had just begun to fall forward, and the usual process was interrupted when she did a fall-catch that reflected her wish to stop and hear what I was saying. I had deflected her relaxed attention to the process and had awakened the volitional process which controlled the fall-catch differently than the reflexive process. When she regained her balance, she explained her responses by saying that she had heard my voice and that she did not want to "let go," meaning give in to the reflexive process. By a complex series of intuition and hypotheses, I made the assumption that this client was indeed intent to hold on to me as the father and that it would take some strong effort to pry her loose from her hold.

This particular weekend afforded the clients the opportunity of having one structure with myself and one with my wife, Diane, as we were co-leading the workshop. The first structure this client had was with my wife, who saw her as withdrawn from the group and a little hostile to the group and the process. At one point following her role as the accommodating parent figure for another member of the group, the client said that she meant nothing that she had said as the good parent and that as a matter of fact cared not in the least for the person whose structure it was. Fortunately for the person whose structure it was, those remarks had little or no effect for as a matter of fact the group had commented that the client had been sensitive and effective in her role as the good parent. It seemed to my wife and to the women in the group that the client was attempting to make them become antagonistic toward her. Clearly, then, her reactions and elicitations of response varied according to the sex of the recipient. From women, my wife and the female client whose structure she tried to dismiss as unreal, she attempted to draw hostility. When it was her turn for a structure, she didn't seem to know what to do and commented that she didn't know how to make demands for herself. My wife mentioned to the client that she seemed to keep to herself and that perhaps she would like to do a structure as a little girl who was playing with her friends in order to give her the opportunity to relate to other people. This early age level was suggested because the client obviously had difficulty relating as an adult and my wife sought an earlier age when perhaps that problem was not yet so pronounced. The client did set up several members of the group as her friends and then had a marvelous time playing as a child with them. Then she commented that it was different and unusual for her to look her "friends" in the face and that it felt good to be able to look at them and have them look at her. She then said that all during the years that she had been in traditional psychotherapy she had never looked at the therapist directly. This was in definite contrast to how she looked at me. Perhaps within the context of the group where my wife sat beside me as I spoke and I was so clearly not going to be available as a sex partner, she was able to express those sexual feelings toward me on some unconscious level. I should have expected her to be sexually seductive toward her therapist, but perhaps since the traditional therapist is an ambiguous figure, he might have been too threatening to look at in that way.

When I saw her in the first session the next morning and asked her what reactions she had to the previous structure, she said that it was wonderful to be young, passive and without responsibilities and how good it felt to have other people running the group who would take care of her. She mentioned that she ran many groups and that it was such a relief not to run this one and that she had purposely worn a little-girl dress this day to keep with the mood of being taken care of and being irresponsible.

The client had seemed to my wife to move in contradictory swings of feelings during her structure. She had made statements unaccompanied by appropriate feelings and then had completely contradicted those statements and had laughed at her contradictions. I already had observed that she was inconsistent in the way she responded and that she seemed ambivalent and relatively "loose" in her expression. Her attempt to carry out the little girl feelings in reality and not just during her own structures indicated to me that she was not making a strict enough separation between structure and reality and therefore that there was an ego problem, for it is the ego that is involved in making that kind of discrimination. This became even more clear during her second structure.

At the end of the group session with my wife, this client, having noted that several structures of other members of the group included some responses to incestuous wishes, remarked that winning your father was no big deal and not worth it. My wife wondered to me if that client had not had sexual relations with her father and wondered if the client would use that material in a structure. Weekend workshops consist of six three-hour sessions over a period of two days, and it was not until the very last session that it was possible for her to have a structure in my group. This particular weekend had long structures and more people than usual who yet had to do structures in the last session. There were six people to be worked with and I spoke with the members to gain a sense of of the issues and priorities involved with each person so that I would be able to pace the time allotments appropriately and to know what kinds of issues might be coming up. When it came to this client's time to speak about her issues or whether she felt much immediate pressure to do a structure, she said that she was feeling very good and didn't need to do another structure.

The plan had been for two groups, my wife's and my own, for which we had alternated leadership, would gather together at the end of the individual structures to work as a single group. The expectation was that we would be ending by ten o'clock or so and by that time her group, which had less structures to do would have joined my group. All five other clients went through their structures successfully and then I turned to the client under discussion and half wondered if she would decline a structure and half hoped that she would as it was now past eleven and I was tired. However I also knew that if she did not do a structure, it would simply postpone to some other time dealing with the material that seemed to be arising. The client said, "I do not want to do anything but I want to say something or announce something that will shock the group." I said, "In that case I think I already know what you might say." She said, "Everybody makes such a big deal about wanting to sleep with their parents; I slept with my father twice in one week when I was twelve years old." She then made a series of contradictory statements to the effect that either it didn't affect her at all and that it stopped her from having the problem that all others in the group seemed to have about wanting to know the parent sexually and feeling guilty about it, to statements or memories that she had suffered such terrible consequences of the act as a child that she could not go to school and study and had terrible nightmares and thoughts that she was a horrible criminal and should be put in prison. She also spoke about being filthy and belonging in the gutter, and she laughed about some of those statements.

I understand the guilt feelings and her wish to shock the group as manifestations of a wish for negative nurturance as punishment for her sexuality and as a substitute for the warmth she could receive from the people in a more appropriate style of relationship. I said to her that I was not shocked and moreover that I felt very sorry for the little girl who had been treated that way and that if I had been her father I would have "kept her in trust" and safe from my or others' sexual explorations until she was old enough to make her own decisions regarding sexual experiences safely and with a minimum of guilt. She laughed when I used the term "keep her in trust" and thought it was a little "ridiculous, cute and old-fashioned." At that point I asked her if she wanted me to be the good father as my wife had just come into the room with the rest of her group which had completed their structures. I suggested that she use my wife as good mother so that we could work with the transference level or reality level with me as well as on the structure level. When I put my arm around my wife and made the usual statement that good parents make at that point, namely, that we only had sex with each other and that I would never direct myself sexually toward her, the client remarked how good it was to see us together and how much she needed to see that.

The structure was not terribly motoric except for some symbolic gestures such as making a circle around her to hold in her sexuality and to keep out too much stimulus from the world. She spoke a lot about what we were saying; at first she would see nothing to it and then she would recall a rapid series of memories that emphasized what we had been saying and that permitted her to consider what the alternatives might have meant to her had she had good parents in her own past. First she said it hadn't affected her to have had her father sexually. I disagreed and pointed out to her that the moment her father had become her lover, she had lost her father as a father, which would have identity consequences. I did not say it to her, but this also meant that she had lost her mother as a mother and had gained her as a competitor. This caused an ego break which permitted her sexual feelings to transcend the parental limitations, an identity crisis when her parents dropped out of their normal roles, and a loss of the limitation and protection normally provided by the parents. She had indeed become her own parents and with great difficulty and with the help of therapy had maintained her balance and her sanity, albeit, with some scars apparent to her ego.

We put our arms around her and said we would protect
her and be her good parents. She said something to the effect that she was strong and didn't need any parents. This
I understood to be the same confusion between structure
and reality that she had made earlier, and I clarified for
her that it was the child we were speaking to and not the
present-day adult. It must have been perfectly clear to her
when we were doing structures with other group members
throughout the weekend that we were responding to the
child memories and not to the reality adult aspect of the
individuals; but in her case she saw the distinctions fuzzily.
When she tried to see what it would have been like to experience strong parents as an adolescent child, she was shocked
to realize that her entire childhood had been transformed
by that event with her father and that she felt she had no
one to turn to at home (she left home and got married at
a very early age). She remembered that she had vowed to
leave home as soon as she could and only at that moment
realized that this vow had to do with the sexual seduction
by her father. Her sexual feelings at this point in her life
were freer than she could really stand, and I believe she
had a lot of guilt and conflict about them. She seemed to
feel it was all right to have sex with anybody and everybody
and really didn't think that incest was harmful, and then
recalled a series of reactions and memories which indicated
that she had suffered terribly from the two incidents with
her father. Slowly she began to accept the ministrations and
protecting and limiting features of the good parents and to
incorporate them into the past and not into the present. This
allowed her to experience a new set of feelings regarding
what her past might have been like.

As the good father I made the gesture of pulling out of
her her father's penis and then demonstrated to her that
I would use my power to protect her and used my hands
to push the world away from her rather than direct my hands

toward her. As I kept repeating that I would not put anything in her, I knew that she would fight because I felt she was dependent on sexuality as the primary relationship mode and did not yet have enough knowledge or expectation of any other mode. She said something to the effect that what good was she if she was not attracting or attractive to me sexually. I replied that I saw her as a sexually attractive person but that I would not direct my sexual expression toward her. In effect she was in the same place as those clients who are being limited in an aggressive limiting structure. If we succeeded we would be stopping the ego break and the availability for guilt to be consumed as a relationship mode with herself and others; we thus would be placing her in a position where she would be able to relate more directly and appropriately with others.

As soon as it became clear that she was beginning to accept the limitations of the good parents and was feeling how it might be to be a safe child in the family structure, she began to talk about how bad she was and to say that she thought people would now be saying that she was a shameful person. I understood that as a wish to consume or relate to negative input, and we set up a negative figure who said she was bad. Her reaction to this was unexpected and interesting. The moment she heard the negative words she made a sucking noise with her mouth as she drew in air and a little saliva. To me it seemed apparent that she was eating the guilt. The good mother said that she didn't have to eat guilt and that she could eat good nurturance from her. The client then remembered and mentioned that her mother had had enormous breasts and that she was always pushing them on her. The good mother said that she would only give her as much as she wanted and would not force her. The client wanted to hear the negative voices again for she heard them in her own mind. Once again she made the sucking sounds and this was transferred over to the mother. We threw away the negative figure and told the client that she was not bad and that she didn't have to eat guilt. Then she felt that the group was thinking that she was bad and that she had also taken up too much time and didn't deserve time in the first place (it was now after twelve). The group responded that they didn't think she was bad at all and that they felt an empathy for her. She wasn't yet able to look directly at the group or have the group look directly in her eyes. We as good parents undertook to protect her from the outside and used our hands as filters to hold back the stimulus from the group. She looked between our fingers at the group and slowly was able to tell us to lower our hands as she related directly to the group. She then felt the structure was over and the group members individually and in groups came to her and she looked at them as they told her how they felt about what she had done.

When a person is very guilty, he responds more to his guilt than he does to anything else in the world. The guilt becomes the target for many interactions and the person relates and interacts with his negative voices inside his own head. One must remember that guilt originates from the deflecting of the energies toward the self. It becomes increasingly clear to me how to understand the dynamics of withdrawn individuals, guilty individuals and ego break individuals in psychomotor terms. How this is put into practice is yet to be seen. This client did not relate well to other people, particularly females in the group, and attempted to receive hostility and guilt voices from them. She very likely related in a sexual way with most men to maintain the sexual omnipotence that was released when she succeeded in sleeping with her own father. However, this pattern was broken in her structure and it is hopeful that it had a more than temporary effect. The fact that she is now in training to be a therapist and that during structures she showed indications that she was sensitive to the needs of others when she accommodated indicates a healthy capacity to overcome her difficulties and to learn new patterns of behavior and reactions.

Negative Voices

All of us at one time or another have felt that we are bad and have heard our thoughts saying just exactly that. I know that when I have had such feelings, they can become so intense that I can think of little else and they take up much of my energy. With psychotic individuals it becomes extreme in that it seems as if the voices are coming from elsewhere than one's own thoughts and the voices have an authority that is hard to disobey. From what we have outlined, it would seem clear that those are the voices of the species ego which is in truth a part of the self. Those patients who have a conversation with their own inner voices are relating to themselves, obviously, whereas they may feel as if they are relating to God or to some other powerful person. With normal or neurotic clients when the voices or thoughts of negative feelings toward one's self become evident, we have attempted to concretize the negative voice as a definite external figure and have that external figure say those negative words. When that external figure says "You are bad," the client or his positive accommodator can attack the negative accommodator, who represents the voice, without attacking the client himself. The client may have conflicting feelings about the voice within himself and wish he could either tear himself up because he is bad or tear the negative voice out because it disturbs him. Neither of these actions is a healthy one. One cannot destroy one's self or tear out a negative aspect of one's self as a therapeutic step. One can, however, place that voice outside in a structure, and then deal with that outside voice without doing injury to one's self.

Let me give an example. This client is a student in his middle twenties who has once been in a mental hospital for a short period of time. He was in the midst of doing some action or having his negative accommodator be beaten up when he began to feel that he was a terrible person. The good parents said, "You are good and don't have to feel guilty about being angry," and he replied that he knew that he was a bad person and had always known it. Whenever a statement comes out that clearly as a complete sentence, it is well to use that sentence just as it was spoken by the client and place it in the mouth of a negative, external voice figure. This is what was done, and when the client heard the statement he smiled and said that it was exactly true. The good parents and myself as group leader said, "Do not accept that voice so readily. Look how much you are enjoying it, eating it up. Fight it off." This he couldn't find in himself to do and therefore it became incumbent upon the good parents to fight off the voice. When the good parents come in at this point it has an interesting effect. Often I have seen a client look at the parents in a puzzled, incredulous way. Sometimes he is shocked to hear someone standing up for him and has an impulsive wish to have the good parents really like him. I suppose the moment a client accepts the ministrations of the good parents, particularly if he believes that they are also strong as well as good, it must put him in a relationship with those parents and take him out of relationship with the guilt processes. When the negative voice sentence is repeated, it might have an entirely different effect. In the case of the student, the second time he heard the sentence he wanted to fight off the negative voice himself, with the help of the good parents. Apparently, a client who reacts in this way begins to want the positive parents to nurture him and relate to him, and he fights off the negative voice as he would any external harmful figure. If the negative voice were not externalized there would be little opportunity to fight against it without tearing one's self apart.

One cannot deal with the negative external voices without also concomitantly having the good parents available because the entire constellation has to be dealt with and not just one factor in it. Psychomotor therapy does just that. It deals with many forces, energies, and phenomena simultaneously on many levels. Suppressing here and releasing there so that the energy disposition within an individual can be dealt with totally and not just in one aspect without dealing with its consequences in other aspects. The earliest uses of psychomotor techniques when the most that we understood was the polarization of the target figures was enough to make for therapeutic progress. The splitting of the figures into positive and negative permitted the safe release of the angry energies without jeopardizing positive relating figures. With the further understanding of the need for limits (which was tacitly inherent in our use of positive figures) and the process of using guilt and species ego energy deflections for negative nurturance, more of the energy phenomena in structures can be explicitly handled. This book's further elaboration of the interactive arena assists greatly in tracking interactive energies and provides a frame of reference which permits a more conscious search for what is going on in a structure.

I would now like to present a chart of the interactive systems including these other factors: body parts, ego perception, ego function, external target, parent function, species ego function, identity statements, normal, pathological. The purpose of the chart is to make clearer the task of knowing what arenas the child has to master before he gains a sense of competence and well-being. It also could assist the group leader or the reader to organize ideas and expectations when observing emotional phenomena.

REFLEXIVE BODY-RIGHTING INTERACTIVE SYSTEM

Body Parts	Ego Perception	Ego Function and Attitudes	External Target	Parent Function
spine, legs, inner-ear balance mechanism, hands ACTION stand walk	perceives weight, touch, muscular effort perceives and recognizes solid objects and the ground	utilizes voluntary movement to modify balance and effort coordinates and times reflexive responses. adapts and modifies reflexes when and if necessary I am different from the ground	gravity, ground hand-grasp-able objects	support child and move child when child cannot for itself withdraw when child fulfills function confirm child's effort and progress

REFLEXIVE BODY-RIGHTING INTERACTIVE SYSTEM

Species Ego Function and Attitudes	Identity Statement	Normal	Pathological
	I can walk	child walks with pleasure and interest	child does not walk
	I can master my balance		does not separate from parents and dependency
			child walks poorly and does not time efforts well

MATERIAL (IMPERSONAL-RATIONAL) INTERACTIVE SYSTEM

Body Parts	Ego Perception	Ego Function and Attitudes	External Target	Parent Function
entire body with emphasis on hands and mouth	perceives shapes, textures, qualities, parts, attributes of things	perceives voluntary control of body	material things	helps child discriminate between qualities of things
ACTION manipulate, handle, analyse, synthesize	perceives the gestalt of things	perceives mechanical gestalt of body as a thing in space		provides child with opportunities to handle and control things
		coordinates and controls body as it controls and manipulates things		confirms child's efforts and progress
		I am different than those things outside me		

MATERIAL (IMPERSONAL-RATIONAL) INTERACTIVE SYSTEM

Species Ego Function and Attitudes	Identity Statement	Normal	Pathological
	I can take things apart and put them back together	child finds pleasure in mastery over and relationship to things	cannot handle, build or control things
	I can build something out of things		people look like things
	I can make things work		things look like people

METABOLIC VEGETATIVE INTERACTIVE SYSTEM

Body Parts	Ego Perception	Ego Function and Attitudes	External Target	Parent Function
mouth, nose, hands,	perceive physiolog- ical states of hunger and air needs.	assist and coordinate when neces- sary, sucking chewing, swallowing breathing eliminating	food, air	feed child until it can feed itself
heart, lungs, sexual organs	perceive and recog- nize food and air through smell and taste	I am differ- ent from food and air		help child discriminate between foods and between food and feces and urine
ACTION eat, eliminate breathe		discriminate between various foods, feces, urine and air		confirm child's efforts and progress

METABOLIC VEGETATIVE INTERACTIVE SYSTEM

Species Ego Function and Attitudes	Identity Statement	Normal	Patho-logical
	I can feed myself and not eat feces or urine	child enjoys eating and eliminating	eating is upsetting eliminating is upsetting
	I can deficate and urinate in the places and at the times I choose		cannot discriminate between food and feces cannot discriminate between food and people cannot feed self cannot control sphincters

VERBAL-SYMBOLIC (INTANGIBLE) INTERACTIVE SYSTEM

Body Parts	Ego Perception	Ego Function and Attitudes	External Target	Parent Function
symbolic thought portion of brain	perception of elements and qualities of thoughts and ideas of self and others	coordinate and modify the flow of thoughts and ideas coming in and going out	own and other people's thoughts, ideas, and symbolic processes	helps child name things and actions and to develop concepts of constructs of ideas
speech center of brain				
mouth, ears	perception of structure and direction of ideas and thought of self and others	I am different than my thoughts and ideas		relates verbally and symbolically to child at its own level
ACTION think, plan, speak				confirms child's efforts and progress

VERBAL-SYMBOLIC (INTANGIBLE) INTERACTIVE SYSTEM
(verbal symbols can be explained as molecular or chemical
miniaturizations or reductions of things in the mind)

Species Ego Function and Attitudes	Identity Statement	Normal	Pathological
	I can manipulate thoughts, ideas and symbols and express them to others	child finds pleasure in mastery and expression of concepts ideas and symbols	cannot think or plan using symbols concepts or ideas

ideas are treated like people

people are treated like ideas |

INTERPERSONAL INTERACTIVE SYSTEM

Body Parts	Ego Perception	Ego Function and Attitudes	External Target
entire body	perceives people as a human gestalt	perceives differences between various people and various parts of people and modifies relation- ships to produce satisfac- tions	other people
ACTION relate physically and emotionally to people	perceives self as a human gestalt		
	perceives relations- ship needs and drives		
	perceives energy outgo and input in relation- ships	coordinates timing, rhythm and expres- sion of inter personal emotions	
		monitors energy outgo and input in relation- ships	
		uses volun- tary move- ment to modify relation- ships	
		I am dif- ferent from other people	

INTERPERSONAL INTERACTIVE SYSTEM

Species Ego Function and Attitudes	Function and Attitudes	Identity	Normal Statement	Pathological
helps child discriminate between people and relationships	shunts energy away from bodily expression if it will injure others	I can handle my feelings I can love people and I can get angry at people without ending my relation ship with them	child enjoys relating with other people	relating is upsetting overwhelmed by own feelings and other's feelings
helps child discriminate between various feelings	other people are like me			people seem to lose their human gestalt
helps child express and control feelings	caring for them and relating to them is like caring and relating to myself			child remains dependent or withdrawn
protects child from over stimulus	hurting people is bad and must be stopped			
confirms child's efforts and progress				

CHAPTER 8

In the psychomotor view living is not just being, it is inter-relating. What in Freudian theory is an instinctive blind bundle of drives becomes in psychomotor therapy one of five interactive energy systems which are inherently target-seeking and somewhat target-knowing. The function of the ego is to assist in the seeking, recognition and matching of the target, and in the coordination of the efforts to achieve appropriate relationships. The ego is to interactive energy as the pilot of a ship is to a ship. The ego may master or control the ship but the ship is not a recalcitrant beast strain-ing to escape its destination. The interactive energy ship wants to get where it is going and the ego helps it get there. "Where id was there ego shall be" is certainly not the goal of psychomotor therapy, at least not in the terms that I un-derstand ego and id. In psychomotor terms the energy sys-tems most available to the ego are the material-impersonal-rational system and the verbal-symbolic-immaterial system. That would mean that if ego took over every function there would be a rather mechanical and abstract symbolic treat-ment of the self without sufficient interpersonal, reflexive; metabolic treatment. The mechanical body would remain but the psychological, interpersonally relating body would be asked to leave.

Actually much of the work in psychomotor therapy seems to me to be the strengthening of the ego, at least in psycho-motor terms. But ego strengthening is a vague term. Cer-tainly I do not mean that the ego made stronger is to take over interactive energy functions. I mean that the ego helps to direct, coordinate, articulate, perceive, and discriminate in all interactive functions to the degree that it enhances the appropriateness and pleasure of the relationship.

There are those who seem to fear the murky dangers of the id. One gathers that the ego must not only keep a firm hand on restraining and distrusting it, but must somehow gain its power and energy and use that power to mobilize the "higher" centers of abstract thinking and symbol manipulation. That seems to me the idea behind the concept of sublimation. The id's sexual energy is sublimated, and that sublimating ability becomes the cornerstone on which civilizations are built. It seems to me that very few major contributors to civilization, such as artists, prophets, architects, philosphers, teachers, urban planners, kings, dictators, presidents were celibates and that puritan societies are not noteworthy as remarkable contributors to the advancement of civilization.

It seems more accurate to me to postulate that the human capacity and propensity for creative, symbolic and abstract manipulations is just as innate and "id-like" as man's capacity to be sexually active and interactive. One does not necessarily have much to do with the other unless disturbances in one interactive system influence the functioning of another. In some views man forces himself to be a man by controlling his animal instincts—that is, if man relaxed he would become an animal. Man is certainly a creature of his own creation—more so than any other species—but man has not "invented" man. This seems to me to be confusing "limiting" as it is understood in psychomotor terms with sublimating or overcoming. Certainly if a man has lived in a nurturant familial surrounding that did not include limitations, there would be potential for destructiveness and chaos, but that does not say that interactive or "id" energies are per se bad or chaotic. As I understand it, the ego is on the interface of interactive energy and is an integral part of that energy system and not inimical or hostile to it. However, if the outside interface is sliced off or not permitted to grow properly, the result cannot be labeled as inevitably bad or uncontrollable, but more as "incomplete."

My impression of psychoanalytic terms and attitudes is that conflict arises between parts of the self and that this conflict possibility is an inevitable part of the human condition. Is it possible that man is bad or angry not because he is innately bad or angry but because he has yet to be in a family structure or society that permits a proper management between his needs and the environment? Psychomotor therapy concentrates on the early family structure and how it influences ego growth and develops patterns of behavior that result in either frustration or satisfaction of interactive needs. In psychomotor therapy the family relations, particularly between child and parents, produce the model from which the ego takes its shape for the future. It is possible that psychomotor definitions of man, his interactive energy and ego phenomena would allow a new understanding of his relationship to the entire universe which would lead to competency and satisfaction in handling relationships on all levels.

The five interactive arenas could be seen as a hierarchy that would lead toward the highest goal of human life, that of an understanding and experiencing of the symbolic and abstract. In psychomotor terms all those arenas would operate continuously, albeit with some changes of emphasis as one grows older. Even though humans do live in an abstract symbolic world a good deal of their adult life, their interactions with other people, things, food, and gravity obviously do not ever stop.

Now let us look at the terms "conscious," and "unconscious." The term "conscious" includes the verbal symbolic arena. It also includes the workings of the ego—yet the ego also includes much that is unconscious. It seems possible to me that there are ego articulations and controls which go on in perfect wakefulness and are not repressed, but of which the individual does not appear to be conscious. This is similar to the way in which an animal, fully awake, makes certain choices, judgments and modifications in its behavior that in a human would be seen as ego processes without that animal being able to "know" that it is making those choices or to verbalize that it was making those choices for certain reasons. Much of human ego processes go on in this way. Unconscious or not conscious in these cases does not mean repressed or id material, it simply means material not yet translated into verbal-symbolic terms for communication purposes.

This would explain so many human actions that are not so much hidden or repressed when they come up in therapy but just plain unnoticed and undescribed by the client, for the processes are not so much verbal as behavioral and have never been translated by that individual into the verbal arena. That would also explain the great disparity one often finds in therapy between what a client says or thinks he is doing and what he actually does. When that occurs it does not necessarily mean that that person whose description of his behavior does not match his actions has been acting irrationally—more exactly, he is acting non-verbally. One would hope that eventually an individual might more exactly describe or understand in verbal terms his actions but that is not necessarily what would make him an emotionally healthier person. Insight is not enough; he must also learn to make and exercise those interactive choices that would be not only more appropriate but more satisfying.

When a person or child attempting to learn to stand and to walk begins to discriminate how much effort to use when, what to hold on to, how much to let his reflexive responses to gravity take hold, how much to contribute in voluntary (material, impersonal, rational) movement, etc., he is using his interactive and ego processes. He may never translate those choices into words. When a child or adult is learning or relearning because of injury how to eat and swallow and what kinds of foods he likes to eat and swallow and to control his eliminatory sphincters and to pay attention to the entire metabolic food interacting system, he is using ego discriminations and modifications but he may find it very difficult to tell you about it. When a child or adult learns which people to come close to and what feelings to give out or take in, he is making ego discriminations regarding the interpersonal interactive arena. He may be called upon to explain his choices or his actions but the reasons he gives need not necessarily be the felt, experienced, or behavioral reasons. The reasons he chooses to verbalize may have a gestalt, a structure and a reasonableness all their own and may represent the capacity of the mind to reason and manipulate verbal symbols rather than explain what actually "happened."

In verbal psychotherapy one may become quite adept at developing a perfect congruency between what occurred behaviorally and what one verbally describes, and that is quite an integrative achievement but not the end of therapy. I have always understood the goal of therapy to be behavioral and perceptual changes that permit a more satisfying relationship with the world as a whole. The disparity between what one thinks and says is going on and what actually is going on is not necessarily a measure of the need for therapy. Words and ideas have their own gestalt and it is surprising how different a person can be in a verbal therapeutic session and in reality. The reality, if it could actually be viewed by the therapist, might not be half so bad as the client describes; in fact it might have little to do with what the client describes.

Psychomotor therapy deals with the actual interpersonal behavior of the client as well as the words of the client. I do not deny the use of words, but I would like to define for the reader and myself the function and use of words in the psychomotor therapeutic setting. Words allow the client to identify his problem and thus help motivate him to change. Words can be useful in re-creating the memory set of a time when certain behavioral choices were made so that those behaviors can be acted out again during the structure of that individual. Words and names are important in identifying the roles of the figures in one's structure so that the appropriate behavioral responses to those figures can be explored. Words are used by the therapist to point out the alternative courses of action available in a structure. However, in all these cases the central focus in the structure is on behavior and experience. The words are in direct relationship to felt behavior and perceived experience and are used to bring to the surface the issues that are present. From my descriptions of cases it should be abundantly clear that words are used extensively in psychomotor therapy. The therapy is not non-verbal in the sense that it uses no words but non-verbal in the sense that the central realities that are dealt with are behavorial and experiential, with the controlled role-playing of the accommodators permitting the actual feelings that would arise with those essential "others" in one's life. Without those accommodating "others" the client would only be able to imagine what he might feel about them in a traditional therapeutic setting without the confirmation of the actual responses and behaviors that arise in a structure. The feelings and behaviors that are aroused in a structure are too concrete to be denied or explained away, and they permit the words that gather about them to be based on emotional realities. If there is a discussion between the client and the therapist in psychomotor sessions, it can have the advantage of a behavioral and experiential structure that both observed, albeit from different vantage points.

Verbal Paradoxes and Contradictions

I have made an argument that the verbal processes are an expression of consciousness, and yet actual experiences demonstrate to me the fact that what a client is saying can be taken in two ways—as a direct and honest statement of where the client is emotionally, or as a rationalization, irrelevant to where I believe he is. If I were to point out to the client the implications of his statement, he might say, "That's what you thought I said; but what I meant was . . ." and add some description that I would consider a denial of what seemed so honest and appropriate. Many times the gist of what I understand as the honest expression is couched in a phrase that seems to have many levels of meaning. There have been times when I have responded likewise and had a conversation with the client on these many levels, with the client responding behaviorally and emotionally to one set of meanings and verbally and rationally to another set of meanings. Those are the times when I can readily believe that there is a person within the client that the client does not know anything about, and that that hidden person is not only visible and present in emotional behavior but sometimes verbally present in the speech of the client without that client's conscious knowledge. Once again, then, we have another meaning for the word "conscious." Before, I took it to mean verbal, and now it is clear that there are times when what is said verbally is also unconscious, or not known or accepted by the speaker.

An example of that would be the verbal interchange between myself and the client I described earlier whom I interrupted just before doing the fall-catch exercise. When she said that she knew that she wasn't going to "let go" and consciously meant that that she wasn't going to be able to relax enough to do the exercise reflexively, I also took it to mean that she wasn't going to let go of the father via holding on to his voice. When I insisted that I would not let her hold on to me, she just as emphatically insisted that she was not going to be able to let go. At the time of this exchange this client had no idea on what level I was talking and responding to her. It was not a knowing, punning, humorous exchange which can be fun to have with a person who is experienced in psychological punning and who knows that both of you are talking on those levels. As far as the client knew, I was just making some cryptic remarks about letting go that she could not understand. It was only later that her "other" meaning became perfectly clear in her structure about her incestuous relationship with her father.

This type of conversation has intrigued me when it has been with some schizophrenic patients who are speaking in a garbled word-salad manner. But with sharp attention paid to poetic or pun meanings, one can "decipher" and talk back to the patient in like manner without presenting anything directly or consciously to the patient. If one did translate one's meanings directly to those schizophrenic patients, there would be either blank denial of or upset responses to what they would consider untenable attitudes on their part. I do not know how to explain this phenomenon in psychomotor terms except to consider that we are seeing the shunting of interpersonal interactive energy to the arena of symbolic verbal expression which is ordinarily the seat of consciousness. To explain how it can remain unconscious while it is being so clearly said is a problem to me unless one postulates a walking, talking "unconscious" that takes up residence in the body. It is not that I do not know what to do with that phenomenon in therapy; I find it very familiar and talk to it all the time verbally and non-verbally, but the difficulty arises in placing it into a theoretical framework that makes sense to me.

Let me give one more brief example of this type of phenomenon in action. It was at a point in the structure where the good parents were together facing the client. The good parents were telling the child that they would never be separated and that they loved the client as a daughter and not as a lover. At some point it became clear that the client was gaining some meaning or satisfaction from the good father's voice which had little or nothing to do with the content of what the father was saying. The client could be said to have been getting nurturance from the father's voice; for she was ignoring the mother as a nurturant figure and had never had a structure where the mother was meaningful as a giving, nurturant figure. Since I was chosen as the good father I said, "I am going to pull my voice out of your ear and I only put my voice into mother's ear." I then leaned over toward the mother figure, placed a hand beside my mouth and her ear and hummed into her ear in a low tone. The moment I made the gesture of pulling my voice out of the client's ear, she rushed both hands to her head with a look of shock and then seeing me and hearing me hum in the mother's ear began crying and saying, "No, no, no." She said, "I don't know what I am crying about but I can't stop. This is ridiculous. I just feel like saying, 'you can't do that to me, you can't take that away from me'." The client thus talked on two levels, one of shock at the loss of the father as a combination nurturant and sexual figure, and the other of surprised observation of her responses which seemed to make no logical sense to her. The client then began to have a feeling of depression and loss and wanted to just curl up and die and be left alone. This is the time when the mother should be made available as an original nurturant figure, and this is what was done. We dealt with some of the client's early, infantile feelings of loss of the mother, and slowly she came to accept this good mother in place of the substitute nurturant voice of the father.

The feelings and behaviors of this client were dealt with in a series of structures dealing with different aspects of the same issues, and she changed in terms of relating to female figures in her everyday life. She also became more of a peer and less of a child to her husband, who was very much older than she. The important point, however, is the disparity between the levels of consciousness and levels of meaning in both her words and her understanding of the words of the good father. On one level the words of the father had a tremendous impact and on another they were ridiculous. On one hand she felt words welling up and said, "You can't do that to me." On the other hand she at first had little idea what she meant by those words or where they came from. Shortly the meanings became perfectly clear and she sought more meaningful relationships with her mother figure. But what is happening during this process? Are we seeing different parts of this client's being come together? How do different aspects of a client come apart and stay apart? How do they come together? The words integrate one's personality, seem appropriate, but what exactly is meant by that? Bringing together these two levels of knowing and of behavior and experience is an important part of therapy, but I have not yet satisfactorily formulated for myself in psychomotor terms what is going on. It is almost as if the personality had the capacity to fragment and to have several pieces of it reside within the self in limited relationship or communication with one another.

One client described a more extreme moment of this kind of occurrence in her structure as like being taken over by a dybbuk. A dybbuk is a demon-type force in some hebrew or yiddish mythology that enters and takes over a person's body for its own purposes. While she was in one of her structures, an exploratory one in which she moved in a motoric, free-associational way without specific targets, she found herself moving in powerful and somewhat convulsive ways and with certain kinds of symbolic and gestural actions that were incomprehensible to her in any context. However, she felt a powerful compulsion to move in those ways. In her case I suppose one can say the fragmented parts had fairly great distance between them. This client has been in a regular weekly group for approximately a year and is still in the process of, for want of a better word, "integrating."

My conclusions are that one can have several "selves" or levels or aspects of one's self residing in one's body and using one's voice at different times. Something can be going on using both one's body and mind, actions and voice, and yet be nameless and unrecognized in the total order of things. Once the process is named and accepted as part of the total self, it can be dealt with more openly and with more conscious direction. I suppose it can be placed in the category of "becoming all of the self," which I postulated earlier in the book as one of the aims of therapy. Something of the above phenomenon can be seen in hypnosis. The subject can be given a suggestion during hypnosis that he will respond to certain words with a certain reaction after he is awakened from the hypnotic state. When the hypnotist says the cue words, the client goes through an elaborate response in exactly the detail he was told to during hypnosis. When asked why he is doing those things, he will be bewildered and unable to find any reason for his behavior or he may present an elaborate explanation that has nothing whatever to do with the real reason. Yet clearly "something or someone" in the subject heard the cue words and responded directly to them. Does hypnosis split off a piece of one's self and place it under the aegis or control of the hypnotist? Who or what is the hypnotist in the cases I have been describing in psychomotor therapy?

The above makes me think of conditioning experiments where a certain cue will produce a result that has no cause and effect relationship and is pretty well outside the animal's or person's conscious control. Are clients conditioned by the events of their past? Are there also some genetic, symbolic conditionings that somehow are triggered in some clients? Consider the infant primate's response to a snake. Experiments have shown that infant primates will respond with remarkable fear to a snake or to snake-like objects even though they have never seen a snake or had a frightening experience with one. Is it possible, then, that we can be hypnotized by hypnotists, by past events and by our own genetic structure? There has been some speculation that mental illnesses can be described as forms of hypnosis, or that they have features that can be explained in terms of hypnotic processes and phenomena.

Perhaps it could be said that one of the jobs of therapy is to assist the client in pulling together under one self or ego all that occurs within the self, so that those aspects of himself that were in control of other aspects or events or one's genetic structure become at least "known" consciously. The client then is able to choose his responses and possibly to modify inappropriate responses. If the client's personality has been "splintered" so that he has more than one self harbored inside his skin, he can be helped to bring it under one leadership.

It is possible that other terms will have to be invented to describe the above situations. Conscious and unconscious do not seem to do the job sufficiently. Perhaps therapy can be understood as education inasmuch as it assists individuals to know how they "work" and, in a sense, to be wakened from the hypnotic trance. Of course understanding and insight are not enough. One has to have the capacity and the motivation to do something with the understanding that would make life more satisfying and meaningful. Meaningful in the sense that we are more than machines or animals frozen in our predestined or pre-programmed slots in the total order of things. It is not all done for the purpose of getting control of everything for it is often enough clear that letting go is sometimes more appropriate than trying, but at least one can know why and choose to let go to processes over which he can never have total control.

Some Unconscious Language

During the years I have been practicing psychomotor therapy; I have come to recognize certain fairly constant or stereotypical body tensions, or actions or postures that allow me to predict the general areas of issues and to assist the client in finding where some of his emotional interactive energy has located itself. These tensions and body postures are important to this chapter in that they indicate the surfacing of an emotion associated with a past experience. The tensions often lead to an active expression of this emotion and a concomitant awareness on the part of the client of the source of the emotion. Thus, is made clear the relationship between the body tensions and actions, the emotions associated with the tensions and actions, and the past experience being recalled. It is this process of a past emotional experience surfacing through body tensions which demonstrates the value of using the body as a route to the unconscious.

When in the beginning of a weekend workshop I have the entire group do the species stance, I ask them to let go of all the muscles that they can in their bodies, without falling down and to attempt to blank their minds of thoughts and feelings. I then ask them to monitor which parts of their bodies call attention to themselves in terms of tension, tingling, pain, or what thoughts they have in terms of potential behavior. When they finish the stance, I ask each group member in turn to report on what he found. Years of hearing these reports and then learning and watching what people do with those tensions has led me to make some rough generalizations about what will be forthcoming. Let me start from the top of the body and then work down to note some of the more common actions and thoughts associated with each part.

Head Tensions

Headaches denote conflict that does not necessarily show up as muscle tension. My first tendency is to think that it is the result of anger that is not finding an appropriate outlet. I don't think of it as repressed sexuality or repressed fear, for headaches almost always seem to have an element of frustration and anger attached to them. When a client speaks about a headache, I may ask him to tighten his fists. Sometimes he will find that his fist tightens strongly and with great power and may follow the tightening with the statement that that effort has made his head begin to throb painfully. The increased pain may make him wish to hold still and remain inactive. However, if that client were permitted to do a structure right then, the anger and the relationships which surrounded the anger would be able to be worked out and very likely the pain and the headache would diminish or disappear. I do not suggest that if one has a headache one should simply make some angry movement. As I explained, that might simply increase the pain. One has to deal with all of the aspects surrounding the anger, with appropriate targets and accommodation in order to change things effectively.

Sometimes the pain of the headache is such that the client may feel like lying down and may state that he doesn't have enough energy to tighten his fists or even to move strongly in any way. Surprisingly, those clients may feel quite energized after doing a structure including some angry expression. It would seem as if the species ego functions in this case to diminish the energy level available in order to control the anger.

The tensing of the body may or may not provoke associations about what is causing the headache. Sometimes the client might get an immediate association about what he is feeling the moment he closes his fist tightly. He may feel he knows exactly who he is angry at and why. If one set up a negative accommodator at that time, the structure could proceed at once. Other times the situation is much less clearly defined and some exploration is necessary.

Eye Pain

Eye pain can also be connected to the expression of anger or to the withholding of the expression of anger. I have at times asked a client who has described or reported eye pain to try to pretend that his eyes were shooting daggers or death rays at the accommodator of his choosing. When the client narrows his eyes, the accommodator reacts as if being pierced, and if this gives the client pleasure and arouses his efforts to continue to narrow his eyes, one can assume that there has been an interactive match achieved. Some clients in this circumstance will become quite excited by the relationship and the accommodation and will begin to walk aggressively toward the accommodator as the accommodator cringes and cries out in pain and anguish at the visual onslaught. Accompanying the client's walking toward the accommodator might be a concomitant tightening of the fists and pursing of the lips in intense grimaces. Some clients have described their subjective feelings at this time and they often included the feeling of an actual flow across space from the eyes to the accommodator. The flow feels relieving to the eyes and is experienced as a real physiological flow. When this occurs I suggest that the client continue to have the same emotional feeling but include some skeletal muscle tightening so that the angry expression becomes more definitely motoric and concrete and less symbolic and indirect. At times clients will profess that they prefer the indirect expression and do not want to tighten the skeletal muscles. Further inquiries as to the reasons for that may lead to responses like, "If I got angry at him with my fists he would just come over and beat the hell out of me because he is so much stronger than I am. This way I have magical power over him and he is helpless." Obviously the client had learned early in his own life that his physical efforts to protect himself were insufficient, and he turned to symbolic means of defense. I am not a champion of brute strength, but it is important for children to learn to be effective and competent on the physical level before they turn to the symbolic, abstract level. I therefore recommend to those clients that they try to use the normal or stereotypical pathway for the expression of anger that would ordinarily flow to mobilize the skeletal muscles. At the very least that would draw the energy away from the eyes, where it cannot be effectively processed, and into the skeletal muscles, where it can be discharged. This demonstrates to me that emotions direct physiological, chemical and neurological messages to the skeletal muscles. If the energy is not processed there, it might flow elsewhere in the body to cause psychosomatic symptoms such as those described in the head or in the eyes.

If I were to tell those clients the moment that they reported the head or eye pain that they were angry, they would probably reply that they were not and ask how I came up with that idea. Yet if the clue of body tension or pain were to be followed out, anger would be the result. Of course it is also possible to pull up anger on demand, just as it is possible to find enough urine for a urine analysis in the doctor's office. The doctor could authoritatively say to the client, "You have to urinate," and the client could honestly reply; "Honest, Doc, I really don't," and, surprise of surprises, find that there really was a little bit of urine in there.

Actually, the parallel would be more apt if the client would tell the doctor, "I have a terrible pain in my lower abdomen." The doctor then would have a greater basis for saying, "Perhaps you have to urinate?" If the client urinated and the pain went away, the doctor would have grounds to assume that there was some relationship between the pain diminishment and the urination. To follow the parallel a bit further the psychomotor therapist might reasonably assume that the head or eye pain had something to do with the expression of anger if the pain diminished following the expression of the anger. The patient in the doctor's office who complained about the pain in the abdomen without himself considering that he might have to urinate would be a rare patient indeed. However, the client in a psychomotor session or in a psychiatrist's office would not necessarily have made that basic connection between anger and his eye and head pain as readily as he would about associating lower abdominal pain with bladder pressure. Most people are not told that they should not urinate and therefore do not have to learn to ignore the signals of a full bladder. Many people have been told that they should not get angry; and they learn to walk around full of anger, with no idea that they might want or need to eliminate it. A backed-up bladder can cause all kinds of consequences further back in the plumbing system, and a backlog of unexpressed anger can do the same to the emotional and perceptional system. It must be said, however, that emotions are not something that one so much eliminates as "processes." Catharsis implies that one eliminates one's emotions much as one eliminates the body's waste materials. Emotions are not waste materials. I have been tempted to think that the emotions were like some fluid traveling around in the body and that sometimes they arrived here at the eyes and caused one type of sensation or action and then could move to the arms and cause another. Wherever the "fluid" seems to be located, the client will talk about that part of the body getting hot or getting itchy, and he will feel some compulsion to use that part of the body in some way. The emotion at times can almost be seen as a thing within a person but separate from the rest of the being that takes over or energizes that part of the body that it settles in. Many of us have experienced a high rage where we can describe the "waves" of feeling coming over us which exerts its own demands on our behavior. During those times one's perceptions of events are not normal and it is only after one finally calms down that the world looks the same again.

Of course, our blood chemistry does change drastically during the experience of emotion, and perhaps there is some way that specific chemicals can gather in certain locales and effect some changes in the behavior of the body at those places. To follow my scheme of interactive energy, this phenomenon would be described as interactive energy changing its mode of expression and target as it moved from one system to another, but it is more than that. What we are describing here is not so much a change from metabolic to interpersonal, although that it included, but a change from one physical mode of expression to another, depending on which part of the body the "feeling" settles in. Sometimes it can settle in the mouth and it will set up a terrific wish and need to bite while in a rage. Before we go any further, it would seem worthwhile to establish a workable name for this "fluid energy," for even if it is only hypothetical, it does describe an existing phenomenon. Let us call it fluid interactive energy.

What is interesting me now is that quite often it is only after the client has begun to move in an angry fashion following the tensing of the fists, that he experiences anger. The interactive energy seems to become evident in body action first and show some external clue to its whereabouts that can be interpreted by a trained observer. Only when he is finally moving does the feeling become known to the person. But that can mislead one to think that one simply has to tense the muscles in order to feel angry; and that is not the case. One first has to have the potential for the anger settled in the muscles. To use my new term, one first has to have the fluid interactive energy in the vicinity, for instance, of the hands and arms. But what has made the fluid interactive energy available in the first place, and what has made it settle at one particular place more than another? What mental or brain agencies or processes are involved in the choosing, and how is it that the individual himself does not know that it is going on until it is well on its way to being expressed?

The answer might simply be found in the mechanisms of interactive energy and their ego processes that I have outlined heretofore and could be entirely unconscious. The selection of one locale over another for the expression of the anger could easily be modified by the environment through conditioning effects and other learnings and become part of the unconscious ego process of selection based on perception both of the internal direction and force of the emotion and on perception of the external direction and force of the target. One explanation of the distance between this type of selection process and the conscious experience and acknowledgement of the feelings that were aroused could be to postulate a conscious and unconscious ego and then one has to explore why they are separate and how they could become more integrated.

The fact there could be such a separation is clinically observable in depersonalized patients in a hospital. Such patients might show signs of physical tension or tingling in a particulare part of the body and then be permitted to express in muscular and motoric ways with the aid of accommodators the behaviors that would be produced by such tension. I have seen such patients express with seemingly tremendous feeling and emotion great amounts of rage or love and then announce in a matter-of-fact tone that they did not "feel" any of what they just did and that it was not representative of themselves. When asked where such powerful feelings came from if not from themselves; they cannot answer. These patients are not lying or hiding from their emotions; they simply are not in touch with them. Their bodies may move but the part of themselves that they consider "me" has not yet been involved or touched nor has it participated in any way with what has been done.

Some schizophrenic patients cannot behave in the muscular motoric way that has just been described. The interactive energy in their cases cannot enter the muscular arena. Depersonalized patients can come in contact with their interpersonal interactive energy on a muscular motoric base, but it is their ego that is split away from the body. That may be the beginning of an answer. Ordinary schizophrenics have had their interactive interpersonal energies shunted away from the body, and depersonalized schizophrenics have had their conscious ego split away or separated from the body. The unconscious ego, in the example of emotional expression that is not felt, is still in relationship with the body, for the structures that these patients are capable of doing, albeit without learning and changing very much, are still in clear congruence with and relationship to their life environment. That is, the emotions are not just explosive and random but follow the same logic and interaction with figures in their lives as any "normal" person's structure would.

The therapeutic approach that I have followed with such patients is to ask them to move their bodies in the usual voluntary exercises while they are controlling their bodies using their conscious ego. The process hopefully will result in the client's saying "I am moving my own body the way I want and I accept that it is my own decision and my own body that is responding to it." I then permit the client to participate in structures that are not emotionally threatening and check whether he is experiencing the movement and feelings or is separated from the movement and feelings. If there seems to be separation, I attempt to knit together, over a period of time, the actions of the self and the conscious ego.

It is clear, then, that my charts have not discriminated between the functions and attitudes of the conscious ego and those of the unconscious ego. The column under identity statement would seem to include the functions and attitudes of the conscious ego. The integrating process that I spoke of earlier would simply mean the linking up or integrating of the unconscious and conscious egos. Most people, when finally energized and mobilized and interacting in an emotional, interpersonal fashion, will accept that the feelings and behaviors are their own. They may be puzzled by them and bewildered by them but they almost always adopt them as their own. So it could be said that a structure is a way of bringing to the surface, or to the doorstep of the conscious ego, the interactive energy of the unconscious ego as only the actions and feelings of the body can do. It is difficult for the normal person to disown all that he feels and sees himself doing unless he is a depersonalized schizophrenic.

If I see the clues of the interactive energy dispersal before it has become activated and then interpret that to the client, he may disown my interpretation, for there is very little feedback to him directly from his own body that would lead him to the same conclusions that I present. My interpretations would point out the separation or distance between the conscious ego and the unconscious ego. The same would be true in a traditional verbal session with a client. The unconscious ego may be communicating clearly to the therapist, through the client's relating of dreams or through his verbal associations, but if the therapist interprets these to the client, the client may have no basis whatever for accepting that information as true or as relating to him in any way. The traditional therapist, just as the psychomotor therapist, has to wait for or arrange for the client to give a more direct expression of his emotions that would permit him to see and accept them as his own. I feel that this is far simpler and more directly believable to a client when he is in a structure than when he is in a verbal therapy session.

When a client is in a structure he knows that there is an outlet for all his emotional expressions and he knows that he will be presented with alternative targets if the ones he is using are not satisfying or are embarrassing to him. He also knows that he is in a structure and not in a reality situation, and he is more willing to "go with his feelings" because he knows that what he is saying and doing has more relevance to past circumstances than to present ones. However, a client in a traditional verbal interaction with his therapist may be forced or feel he is being forced to accept attitudes and feelings toward the therapist that are unacceptable to his "now" assessment of himself. I can see where a client would have enormous resistances to such feelings and information about himself, even if it is made clear to him that these are old feelings and not representative of his adult assessment of himself. The traditional verbal session is sometimes so arranged that the client has to "really" believe that the therapist is behaving like his original mother or father before he can integrate his feelings toward his parents into his conscious ego. The structure as a therapeutic device permits this kind of learning with more opportunities for finding alternative forms of behavior and response.

Review of Terms

I would like to expand on the terms "conscious" and "unconscious ego." It seems to me that what I have often understood as unconscious and assumed to be of unconscious origins can be placed under the catergory of unconscious ego. The term "unconscious ego" might also well be understood as "body ego." A child, after all, makes the most of his gravity, metabolic, interpersonal interactive matches well before he is proficient in speech. It is not surprising then, that he has so few words or concepts available to deal with or describe what he has done. And if he is told that some way of relating which he has found to be satisfying is wrong or inappropriate, he may not learn to recognize it consciously and continue to do it without knowing it. Repression in this case would not be repression of the action but repression of the conscious knowledge about or experience of the action (and also repression of the knowledge of the potential for the action). Yet that cannot be the only process at work, for the verbal ego is certainly *also* representative of the individual rational self. However, the verbal conscious ego may operate within a fairly wide range of congruence with the unconscious or body ego. What is needed is an understanding of and explanation for the development of relative distance between the two kinds of ego. My experience shows me that most normal people have pretty impressive distances between their conscious and unconscious egos, and how is that to be explained and how is their "normalcy" to be explained? How is it possible to lead such body- and emotion-blind lives and still remain in one piece and lead relatively satisfying lives? In some respects it makes the conscious verbal ego seem irrelevant, and yet that is what makes a human different from other animals. What is the point of having a conscious verbal ego if there can be so little dysfunction in the living process and so little personal discomfort even if the verbal conscious ego is far away from emotional reality and relevance? Or are we all living in an unconscious despair whose extent is measurable by the distance between our conscious and unconscious egos?

Can this explain why realizing our human potential is something that is striven for and not often attained? Then being human does include the inevitability of conflict due to the psychic structure of man's two ego states. Not the conflict between the id and ego or superego but the conflict or possibility for incongruency between man's conscious and unconscious egos.

The question remains: how important is the conscious verbal ego for human living? What are its limits and uses? Is this distance between the two egos at all valuable, even while it creates such a large potential for conflict and incongruity? My immediate answer to this last question is a resounding Yes. Sometimes a good white lie to one's self will let life go on whereas the truth might cause impossible suffering, and possibly the end of life. How is it that life cannot stand to know the truth about life? The problem, then, is to find the basis for the standards of the conscious verbal ego and how it is that these standards can be in such contrast and contradiction to actual human living realities. In other words, how is it life and ourselves as living creatures can tolerate world views, religions and philosophies that contradict what we know interactively, emotionally and non-verbally to be true? What kind of knowing is it when we *"know* it to be true" and yet deny it consciously? It must be a kind of knowing that can be denied, subjugated, subverted and discarded. Then which knowing is the more superior and the more valuable, that of the non-verbal, experiential, unconscious body ego, or that of the symbolic, verbal, conscious ego? However much the non-verbal, unconscious ego is subjugated or denied, it must have its needs met on some level or in some way or the person will literally physically die. It may have its needs fulfilled in the numerous ways noted earlier in the section on interactive energy, but it is the verbal ego that calls the shots—or is it?

Perhaps answers can be found by looking at the developmental process to see when the capacity and need for the activation and growth of the conscious verbal ego arises. I realize that until now I have taken it for granted that when I used the term "ego," that there was nothing other than body ego although I hadn't called it that. I described the ego as much like a skin or interface of interactive energy that moderated the interactive matches between the self and the rest of the energetic world. The ego filtered the energy input by assessing the quantity and direction of environmental energies and accepting or avoiding or rejecting them. The ego also was described as a filter that would modify and direct the internal energies so that the skin and the self were not burst by the force of one's feelings. The protecting and limiting functions of the parents were understood to be important factors in developing those capacities in one's self. The functions of the ego; therefore; were to perceive inner and outer energy distributions and directions, modify and direct the interactive forces to maintain the economy and continuity of life, and thus to ensure the proper functioning of one's interactive arenas and to satisfy one's interactive needs.

Now if the verbal, conscious ego does indeed exist, its functions must be very much like the functions of the body ego but operating on the conscious, verbal-symbolic level. Earlier in the book I described the possibility that certain types of pathology arise from the capacity to symbolize and to treat symbols as real. When that process was used in place of the actual support and nurturance provided by the real parents, and those needs were met in an abstract, symbolic way by the self, life became that much less real and less satisfying, and there was less satisfying interaction with other people. I also wrote that there was a verbal-symbolic interactive arena and that one learned to make verbal-symbolic matches just as one learned to make other types of interactive matches. From this, I present the following two suppositions: there is a verbal symbolic conscious ego, just as other interactive energy systems have ego interfaces to moderate the energy distribution; and, there is the human capacity (and developmental need) to treat verbal symbols as if they were real. Therefore, I must assume that the human organism grows and develops from the motoric-muscular interactive state to the abstract, symbolic-verbal state. The verbal symbols are just as real and manipulable as one's own body and limbs. It is clear that one cannot heal, teach or "therapize" a human without paying strict attention to his verbal as well as to his body ego.

The human being, then, by virtue of his genetic, developmental structure, prepares to live a portion of his life in the verbal-symbolic arena, which affects with all the power of the concretely real his metabolic, muscular interactive life. His verbal-symbolic ego must have a structure that functions to keep the individual properly balanced between his inner self and the outer world. One of the implications of this is that one can shear off the verbal-symbolic ego by using verbal symbols and leave the interactive energy without the ego and therefore undirected and without limitation.

Let me give some examples of this type of phenomenon. I have read that some people who are allergic to certain types of foods, when told (falsely) that they had just eaten that food would develop all the symptoms of the allergy; that is, the verbal symbols were enough to trigger metabolic responses, the verbal symbol became as real as the irritating food. It is important to note that there can be great disparity between what is actual and concrete and what is verbally described, and yet the result can be the same as if it were actual. The same kind of phenomenon can be seen in hypnosis; a subject can be told that he is like a dog and enough dog-like behavior is elicited to make one see that some part of that person believed the verbal symbols and was prepared to "live them out." Apparently, in hypnosis the hypnotist takes control of the subject's verbal ego and uses verbal symbols to manipulate his responses. One should note that if there were continuous disparity between the actual and the symbolic—that is, if a subject under hypnosis were constantly fed symbolic information that contradicted concrete, metabolic reality—it would very likely produce some kind of disturbances. The same could be said of non-hypnotized people whose verbal-symbolic ego was at odds with their body ego, which more likely represents concrete reality.

The verbal-symbolic ego of a person must operate by developing, during his early maturation, a set of symbols and words to represent external reality and a similar set of symbols and symbols and words to represent his self. That is, interactive energies of all kinds—reflexive, metabolic, interpersonal and material—would have key words, symbols, and concepts attached to or representing them. The external interactive forces and energies of the world and the internal interactive energies of the self, symbolically represented, would be moderated by a verbal-symbolic representation of the body ego or the self. Then if all went well, the entire interactive process, or most of it, could take place on the symbolic level exactly as the body ego moderates, modifies, monitors and filters concrete motoric, muscular interactive energies. Yet one can immediately see the pitfalls that such a transposition could entail. The interactive energies of the world, the self and the ego functions could be accidentally or purposely misnamed, misunderstood or not be given a name at all. Any of those errors would have consequences and one simply has to look around at the world at large to see them. The naming process that little children go through should be carefully and clearly articulated, for those things left unnamed could be left in a symbolic limbo and real objects, energies or functions could be treated as if they did not exist, even though they had concrete, tactile reality that could be experienced by the body and body ego. This would certainly provide a person with cognitive and other kinds of dissonance! And isn't this what we therapists see every time we work? What if there were no names given to the sexual organs and they were never talked about in one's home? Wouldn't that be an effective way of making sex go underground? How could one deal with one's sexual feelings? One would have to learn to depersonalize, tolerate psychic disharmony, develop new words and concepts, psychically or actually perform a genital removing operation or in some other way resolve the confusion.

Parents should be careful not to give certain kinds of pet names to their children or to bodily functions of their children for they will live out the implication of the names. To return to the hypnotist making a person act dog-like, I remember a mother whom I knew (not therapeutically) who often said to her daughter, "You are so stupid I should have sent the dog to school and kept you at home," implying that she was not as intelligent as the dog. That poor child grew up with her self-esteem impaired and looked less pretty and more "hang-dog" as the years went on. Since it is the parents who do most of the early naming and sanctioning of behavior, it is their function to see to it that the child does not grow up with an impaired verbal-symbolic ego. Not only do the parents name objects and functions of the outer interactive universe, but they name the child and his own interactive functions and also directly and indirectly *sanction* those functions. (Interestingly, children who are born out of wedlock either do not have a legitimate name or have a "mark" on their name. Also, people are often concerned with not losing their good name). The child's self-esteem could relate to what he is called and how he is treated as well as to how well he lives up to the frames of reference established by the parents and the society in which he lives. Thus the parents have a great responsibility on the verbal-symbolic level. I have previously been well aware of how tremendously important it is that the parents meet the interactive needs of the child, but I am now emphasizing the importance of the parents' role (and, I suppose, that of the school system as well) in developing the child's verbal-symbolic picture of the world and of himself.

There are various ways of coping with this disparity. For example, the need some people have to combine liquor and sexuality leads me to think that they must have to deaden their verbal-symbolic egos before they can function sexually, for sexual organs and behavior may never have been properly named or sanctioned in their homes or cultures. Perhaps this is also why some people have to have sex in the dark, for then they may be able to deny that they are having it, and also why some people may have to depersonalize in order to have sex. I suppose some people may have to deny or depersonalize the functions of eating and eliminating because those functions may never have been properly named or sanctioned. They certainly could not stop doing those things or they would not be able to continue living, so they must have to be able to create and maintain a distance between the body ego and the verbal-symbolic ego in order to maintain life itself.

This demonstrates clearly the power and function of words in the process of clarifying what one is doing and how to continue to change one's behavior. One of the functions of good parents is to name the interactive events and sanction them and verbally clarify them, as well as to meet the interactive needs of the child.

In our psychomotor structures we give names to processes which a client is incapable of symbolizing verbally. We permit the surfacing of the interactive energy under the aegis of the body ego. By having the good parent name and sanction the behavior as it is acted out we are healing the distance between the body ego and the verbal-symbolic ego. By using words and symbolic concepts to describe the person's actions and behaviors which were established and articulated before words and their clarifying function were available, we are bringing to the body ego and the motoric interactive process the clarifying assistance of the verbal ego. In other words in the last process we are bringing out into the open, in terms of overt behavior, patterns of interaction which might not be entirely satisfactory and are unconscious and unnamed and thus we are "maturing" or improving the body ego matches. We have in a structure the opportunity for going back and re-educating the body ego by using discriminations and controls that were not available in the first enactment. For instance, when a client is undergoing a rebirth structure he has available not only his own verbal-symbolic ego, which is monitoring and watching the process, but the verbal-symbolic egos of the group leader and the rest of the group. The client, when he was actually being born, did not have available his own symbolic-verbal ego, and even though his mother's or the doctor's or the nurse's ego was present, he was not able to be in communication with it. If in reality the child was under pressure at birth and experienced discomfort and pain in the event, or if the child was not sufficiently cared for after birth and was lonely and frightened, he can now in a structure be told as *both the child and the adult simultaneously* that his good mother loved him and that both parents wanted him and were looking forward to his birth. He can be assured that when he was being pressed on from the outside (by the accommodators in the structure and the uterine canal during his birth), it was not being done to hurt him but to help him move and be born, and that when his mother nursed him it was her breast that provided the milk, that he was not eating his mother, that his mother liked feeding him, and so forth. The labelling and naming process would tend to change the tension of the original event and make it more understandable and manageable, and would more effectively co-ordinate the interactive matches. This is particularly so in structures dealing with a later period of the client's life. The client not only is held by the good parents but is told that they are supporting and protecting him, making the experience much more clear and understandable.

Thus a structure is not only an arena for satisfying unmet interactive needs, making clearer interactive matches, placing interactive energy in the appropriate energy systems and arenas; it is clearly also an arena for the integration of the two kinds of egos and for the development and maturation and articulation of those egos.

I am increasingly aware of the enormous complexity of the human being. I will try to list for myself and the reader the frames of reference, scales or gauges that can be checked out when a therapist is confronted with a client and is attempting to find out not only something about who he is but something about what his problems are and some way to understand them and organize an approach that would lead toward a solution of those problems. This is something of a checklist for the psychomotor therapist:

1. What are the areas showing body tension.

2. What are the kinds of behavior the client associates with those areas.

3. Can the client translate the tensions into action.

4. What is the action that results.

5. Is it being expressed via the appropriate motor system.

6. Can the client name the action.

7. Does the action relate to anger or frustration and for what reason.

8. Does the action relate to any interactive deficits.

9. If so, what interactive system and at what age level.

10. Does the client have a name for the target of his action.

11. How does he react when the name is used. Does he accept or reject his target or the name of it.

12. Can he believe that the negative parents were wrong in treating him badly, or does he feel that he is unworthy of fair treatment.

13. Can he accept the ministrations of the good parents.

14. Does he show changed behavior as a result of his structures, or does he remain the same. If so, why.

It is time to return to the tour of the body regarding the meanings and potential behaviors behind certain areas of tension.

CHAPTER 9

More about the Eyes

There are times when a client will move his hands over his eyes without making any comment about pain or tension in his eyes. Depending on how this is done, it can have different interpretations. Sometimes it is a gesture that looks exactly as if a tear is being wiped away and is simply interpreted as such. Of course there are times when the client is simply rubbing the corner of his eyes to remove dust or whatever, but if one monitors the gesture and the statements and the emotional tone of the client, it can often be found that he is grieving or feeling sad about some aspect of what he is describing. The indications are that if the client were to become more aware or conscious of his feelings regarding the topic of conversation or description, he would actually find that he wished to cry. Often it is not worthwhile to tell the client, "You are sad about something," for he is not yet experiencing the sadness. The therapist can note the fact that there may be sadness or grief regarding the subject under discussion and perhaps be on the lookout for some future expression of that feeling, giving it a name and sanctioning it as well, for if the client is a man, he may feel that it is not manly to cry and must be assured that to do so would not diminish his self-esteem.

The other gesture concerning the eyes is more energetic and has less obvious associations. The client in this case may rub his eyes very forcefully, virtually digging his fingers into them and then massaging them in a rotating movement. Sometimes it looks like the gesture that some people make when they are very fatigued and their eyes are aching and tired. Often, fatigued eyes may be all that is being indicated, but I have become impressed and intrigued with how often such a gesture points to or is associated with sexual guilt. I don't presume to know how such movement and such ideation come together, but it seems to me no accident that Oedipus plucked his eyes out when he learned he had murdered his father and slept with his mother.

If sexual guilt operates at all like aggression guilt, the species ego turns the energy back upon the self in order to deflect it from going out to some unacceptable figure. One might speculate that the fingers of the client rubbing his eyes represent the penis and his eyes represent the female genitals, and that the entire gesture could be a symbolic rendition of having sexual relations with one's self in order not to have it with one's parent. The other association the gesture has for me is that the eyes themselves may represent the penetrating male penis and the fingers might be used to blot them out and stop them from their penetrating drives. This gesture is observable in both male and female clients.

The idea that sexuality turned toward the self might be a species ego function to deflect the energy away from a forbidden figure makes me wonder if male homosexuals, many of whom are raised in a male-less home (giving rise to all kinds of sexual omnipotence in my frame of reference—dad is gone or weak, mom is all for me), do not include some deep-seated sexual guilt about their mothers in their personality structures. It could be stated this way: in order not to penetrate mother, the male homosexual perhaps experiences an energy deflection that points his penis toward himself via the person of another male. At least then his homosexual adjustment permits a seeming relationship with another person rather than only relating sexually with himself via masturbation.

While we are on the subject of sexual guilt, some female clients represent what seems to me another species ego function, that is the energy-drop method of restraining a forbidden impulse. This shows up more often in structures than during exploratory exercises or conversations. If in the structure the father figure for some reason becomes separated from the mother and seems even momentarily available to the daughter, she may suddenly feel the room spinning and feel that she is going to faint. I have learned to react to that by placing the good father very close to the good mother and having him state firmly and unequivocally that no matter what the daughter feels toward him (and it is all right for her to feel sexually toward him), he will never be available to her as a sexual partner. It is useful to have a male contemporary figure available for the female client so that her fiercely turned off sexual feelings, if released and directly experienced, could be given an appropriate and acceptable target. Of course it is not likely that the female client will experience sexual feelings at this time. She is very probably thoroughly terrified of them and is struggling to get them under some kind of control. As is our practice in psychomotor therapy, when there are omnipotent feelings that have burst beyond the ego's capacity to control, one can deal with this by doing a limiting structure—in this case limiting the sexual power of the daughter. When the client is ready, and it may be some time in the future, she may undergo a structure where she attempts to seduce the father away from the mother, using all her wiles and cunning and even her aggressive attempts to pull the father away from the mother. When the daughter's sexual energy is aroused by the good father and he is safely unavailable, she can then express her feelings and have them limited and given an alternate target. Frequently the so-called sexual energy is a means of close relationship with the father in compensation for poor early relationships with a non-nurturant mother.

The Ear

The most obvious use of the ear in a session is, of course, as an organ of hearing. There are times when a group member might not want to hear what either the good or the bad parents are saying, and he might unconsciously place his hands over his ears to shut out the message. Playing with the ears or poking fingers or objects into the ears might indicate a wish to be entered or penetrated.

Little children love to share secrets with each other, and I am sure this has to do both with the reality of hearing and with the symbolism of intimacy and sexuality that is experienced around the ear. All the sense organs that are involved with a direct and obvious "taking in" of reality or the outside world or external stimuli could easily be understood by the body ego as a means of entering the self. This can be an entering that is desired and be a part of living such as the entering of food into the mouth, or any energy into any sense organ that enhances knowledge, control, satisfaction and pleasure in life. Or it can be a forced entering and be seen as an ego break, an invasion, or a rape.

If there is something that is outside that one does not wish to see, one simply closes one's eyes. It is a bit more difficult to hold out an offensive odor, for one has to breathe in order to live, but one can temporarily hold one's breath. But one cannot turn off hearing, for there are no ear flaps as there are eyelids. Sounds can only be held out by placing one's hands or some other object over one's ears.

It seems important to me to note how people relate to their organs of sensory input. For how one deals with external stimuli says a great deal about how one's body ego is functioning. How discriminating is the client about what he permits to come into himself? Is he able to enjoy tasting and smelling, or do all odors seem equally distasteful? Does he like to hear music and can he discriminate well between varying sounds so that he is not merely a glutton for sound but can distinguish nuances and derive pleasure from the variations and relationships between the sounds? That is, how articulated is his body ego as it is represented by his ear?

Is the ear an organ for receiving nurturance, for receiving sex, for receiving invasion? Does he relate to the world of sound with pleasure or with aversion?

Some female clients, when they have their own contemporary who will whisper or hum into the ears, are transported with pleasure and seem to relax and enjoy the whispering. Others cannot seem even to permit the mouth of their contemporary to get very close to their ears and become tense and jerk away from the contact and the sound. The negative response to the whispering and the touch can be modified if the situation is made clear, and if the stimulus is approached gradually. It should be made clear that it is the contemporary who is whispering and not the father and that the sound will not be forced into them but extended to them only to the extent that they wish it to be.

The Nose

I remember that as a boy my age group and I had a gesture that we all understood and used when we were showing that we were ready to fight, either seriously or in a mock battle. We would bounce about with the dancing footwork of a boxer, raise our hands in the standard boxing pose and brush our right thumbs across our noses, and simultaneously make a slight snorting sound by taking in a breath. We probably had seen this done in the movies, either seriously or in a slapstick manner.

The nose still seems to be an indicator of aggressive drives. Whenever a client rubs his nose and looks warily about, I feel that he is possibly apprehensive and ready to be defensive and do battle. But there is an entire language about how one uses one's nose, and certainly I am not indicating a one-to-one relationship between nose touching and aggressive intent. When any expressive element is perceived, such as rubbing one's nose, all other elements must be looked at as well because it is the totality that contains the message, and that message is very complex. The nose also has male or phallic sexual symbolism; and this can be combined with the aggressive implications to shade the overall meaning. The nose seen as a phallus by the body ego could account for some clients' stroking their noses. In those cases the nose is stroked and sensitively caressed and the meaning seems more masturbatory than anything else. The common verbal understanding of nose rubbing includes "itchy nose, itching for a fight," but it could also mean itching for sex, and obviously sexuality and aggressiveness are quite intermixed.

One female client described earlier as having sexual feelings toward her mother that gave her great guilt had a habit of cleaning her nose in a very particular way that I have not seen before. She would take a piece of Kleenex and place it over her finger and then poke her finger into her nose. The usual action includes poking around up in the nose for mucous and then pulling the hardened mucous down. In her case she seemed more interested in mucous at the lower end of the nostril for she seemed to be pushing her finger forward and slightly down. If her nose had been made of elastic material she would have stretched it until it was quite a bit longer than it was. The gesture was not done gently but was vigorous, energetic and frequent. I interpreted it to myself as a possible wish to elongate her maleness via the phallic nose. However one interprets is of little consequence unless one also finds some way of dealing effectively with the phenomena or the interpretation. My response was to give her the message from the good mother that she did not have to be a boy in order to be loved and that the good mother could and would love her just as she was, as a girl.

As in many other symbolic gestures and actions the energy focuses on the organ or body part in question with little or no conscious awareness of the feeling; however, the verbal associations of the client should be noted by the group leader as they often have relevance to the action. For instance, if a male client is talking about another male and at the same time is rubbing his nose, it is possible that he may be feeling either hostile or sexual toward that male. My tendency would be to guess that the client's feeling includes sexuality if he is caressing his nose and aggressiveness or hostility if he is rubbing it forcefully. Of course, there is no hard and fast rule regarding this for it is also possible that the nose rubbing has nothing whatever to do with verbalizations that a client is making. One's nose sometimes itches with no other meaning than that it itches. However, frequently enough it can indicate the possibility of other feelings and emotions, and the therapist should monitor the client's behavior and speech in a relaxed state of mind so that any combination of verbal and body messages would not slip by him and yet not be forced by him. A therapist could suggest certain interpretations to a client and produce those feelings in the client by the power of suggestion alone, so it is important for the therapist to "stay loose" and not to push onto the client those feelings which he guesses are there and which are not in reality there. One must also keep in mind that the therapist might well be right about an interpretation even while a client might reject such notions vehemently should the therapist share his interpretation with him. Clearly, it is no easy task to glean reality, whatever it is, from the mixture of projections and guesses by the therapist, denials from a client and what might actually be felt. What is felt is also not clear, for as we learned in the previous chapter, what one experiences is not at all what one might feel on other levels. One sometimes experiences an emotion only after one behaves in response to that emotion, so that a therapist can sometimes assist a client to recognize an incipient feeling by pointing out that such and such a gesture or movement is being made by the client. The client then has the option of permitting that feeling to become overt and experiencing the emotion. There is clearly a fuzzy area where it is uncertain whether a client is experiencing an emotion because the therapist suggested it, or whether the therapist is correctly assessing a symbolic body tension or action and is really helping the client integrate this feeling with his actions.

Another way to use the information that is accumulating when a client is rubbing his nose is to ask the client to note the quality of the feeling in his fingers and nose and then to touch someone else with this same quality of feeling. That is, the client is asked to direct the interactive energy away from his nose to another person. Another possibility would be to have someone else selected by the client rub the client's nose the way he himself was rubbing it. In any event the energy is given the possibility of an external target, with the client's determining who the target should be. An entire structure can be developed from this point to find out what the energy is that is being expressed in this way, who the target is, and whether it is the appropriate one.

Sneezing is sometimes indicative of sudden and strong sexual feelings. Strangely, the feelings are not experienced genitally, but the sneeze often occurs when a male client is potentially highly stimulated. I understand the sneeze to be rather like a nasal orgasm and indicative of the potential or wish for a phallic orgasm. In this respect the taking of snuff and the subsequent sneezing can be understood as a nasal masturbation and climax. This may sound far-fetched, but often enough sneezing has directly pointed to sexual wishes that would not otherwise make an appearance, for instance, where a client might have sexual feelings toward a mother or daughter figure and might find it difficult to accept or experience those feelings directly.

Sneezing of course, is often the result simply of dust or of cold or hay fever. Whatever it is that causes sneezing there is no doubt that the nose has a function of its own, and that is to breathe and detect odors. How one uses it on that level is just as significant as how it might be used on the body-symbolic level. Does one breathe easily or is one's nose stuffed all the time? Stuffed in this case being possibly an expression of trying to hold the world out even at the expense of not breathing. How do people enjoy or not enjoy odors? How important is the nose in learning about the world? I am reminded of an autistic boy I worked with some years back. He had the habit of smelling everything that interested him. It was as if smelling between odors was the level to which his body ego had advanced. In terms of my schema he was relating primarily at the metabolic level. Even though he was twenty years old, this patient could not communicate verbally very well and most significantly could not do voluntary movement at all. By that I mean that he could not move his body in the voluntary modality used in psychomotor therapy where a client decides how he is going to move his body and then moves in that manner with no other purpose than to have mastery over his body. This patient did not understand the concept of front, side or back, and I frequently would move his arms in various directions, naming the directions verbally as I moved him in the hope that slowly he would gain control of the behavior and concepts on a voluntary level. This he did to a small extent before he was transferred to another hospital.

This patient learned to increase his skill in working with materials in occupational therapy, and this was an important part of his progress. He did have some use of words and could recite poems he had learned when he was much younger and other sayings that were drilled into him by the other patients in the hall. However, as I said, he was fascinated most by how things smelled and was constantly placing objects to his nose and sniffing them. When I asked what one of these objects smelled like, I was startled and amused when he said "pussy." This response had been taught to him by some of the patients as a joke. It is interesting, however, that he did not use other responses people tried to teach him with the same constancy and tenacity as the word "pussy"—a slang expression for the female genitals. I heard him say this many, many times as people frequently asked him what he was smelling. He seemed to have some idea of the meaning himself because he would often giggle after saying it. Of course, the giggle could have come from the often shocked and amused reaction his word produced in others. However, he did have sexual feelings, for the hall staff told me that they were forever trying to stop him from masturbating and pulling on his penis. When working with him, he would say that he had to "weebee," his way of saying weewee or urinate and I would accompany him to the toilet. He would take quite a bit of time urinating and much of it was spent playing with his penis.

To follow the nose-penis combination or relationship a bit further, in the animal world the nose is one of the most important sensory organs. For fish this is the most important sense for it tells where food is and in mating season where one's opposite is. In the animal world it is the nose that tells one where one's lover is and whether she is ready or not for sex. It is indeed the nose that tells the male about the female genitals when the female is in heat. It is not the female behavior that draws the male dog, but the female scent. That is, he is attracted to his mate with his nose and not with his eyes. Therefore the nose is indeed responsive to sexual stimuli. What is the function of perfume if not to arouse sexuality? Yet some perfumes make one feel like one would like to "eat the girl up" rather than have sex with her. The nose is indeed used for making food discriminations as well as for making sexual discriminations.

The Mouth

The mouth is at once the seat of the most primitive act of being and in man the seat of the most advanced act of being. The mouth is used for both eating and speaking. Let us add up the functions of the mouth: tasting, chewing, swallowing, touching (that is with the tongue or lips), breathing and speaking. For some animals one could add lifting, supporting or carrying and manipulating. Some species of fish protect their young by holding them in their mouth when a predator comes by. Birds feed their young by placing food in the beaks of their chicks with their own beaks. The mouth, then, has sensory functions as well as metabolic functions; the mouth makes taste discriminations during the beginning of metabolism when the food is chewed and combined with digestive juices in the mouth.

Other sense organs such as the ear or nose have no interactive or manipulative functions except in symbolic ways as described above, but the mouth does in fact have those functions. Therefore, the mouth has interactive energy functions as well as ego functions (ego functions in that any sense organ has a discriminating and therefore ego function). The mouth operates in all the interactive energy systems except the reflexive gravitational. It obviously operates in the metabolic system in eating; the interpersonal system in kissing, caressing and speaking (in animals cleaning and grooming); and the material system in manipulating things (including the manipulation of symbols in speech). It is as if all of the self were focused around the mouth except for the ares of sexuality, elimination and gravity (although in the first two the mouth does have functions, for instance, oral sex and vomiting).

The mouth, then, is an important part of the entire being and it can be hypothesized that all of life began with the mouth and elaborated out from it. If the skin of the self is like the body ego then the mouth is the most important aperture in the ego and that goes for the body ego as well as for the verbal-symbolic ego. I have often used metabolism as a model for further elaborations of life including thinking and now I see the organic base for that thought.

When we look at the kinds of movement and incipient or symbolic behavior regarding the mouth in structures, we must keep in mind the wide range of functions the mouth has in order to place the action in the correct frame of reference. Quite often when a new group of people has completed the species stance at the beginning of a weekend workshop, some will comment that they feel a tension in their jaws and seem to wish to bite down hard on something. When those people are given an accommodator, it becomes clear whether they really wish to bite by their response to the accommodation. For instance, if he is given a female accommodator who responds to his biting down hard, the client may find that her voice is not the one he wants to hear. If he is then given a male accommodator and that response pleases him, we go on from there and have him name the figure his accommodator represents and then learn where he is biting him.

The biting can have all kinds of meanings, from biting off the nipple of the negative mother to biting off the threatening penis of the negative father. It might also be simply a matter of holding on to either parent with the teeth instead of with the hands. It can possibly be a gnashing of the teeth in frustration with no specific target. Sometimes the tension in the jaws is a result of the client's holding on to his own feelings, that is, keeping his feelings from coming out via the mouth. That may be a way of holding in the words that he might not wish to say out loud. However, it is more likely that word retaining shows up more in tension in the lips and not in the jaw. Clients who are holding back words might also fleetingly cover their mouths with their hands, or literally hold the mouth shut with the hand or fingers.

Fingers being held to the mouth is a common gesture and regularly has a meaning associated with nurturing. In moments of uncertainty a client will put his fingers to his mouth and even make sucking movements and sounds with his lips on his fingers. The good mother is offered as a possible target for those feelings. The force of the movements of the mouth is indicative of the type of feeling that is being expressed. Sometimes the mouth is pursed as if to say "No, I won't," in a stubborn manner. At other times it appears as if the mouth is being closed in order to keep food from being forced into it. The associations that the client has about the action are important, for only then can the appropriate setting be arranged for a structure. Food forced into a child is much like any other invasion—the child who resists is not being simply stubborn, he is fighting for his sovereignty. If the mother succeeds in breaking through his ego via his mouth, he is therefore capable of being entered and manipulated on the symbolic level as well. That kind of upbringing by the mother would make it difficult for that person to take in all other kinds of reality and stimulus.

Sometimes the mouth is moved in a way that seems to indicate expulsion. The air may be blown out of the mouth, and if the blowing is accommodated to, the client may find that he wishes to expel something from within him through his mouth. It is possible that this is the same client who was pursing his lips and is now spitting out the negative invasion of the mother. If the client receives satisfying accommodation to his gesture of blowing out, he may begin a shouting, vomiting expulsion, and the accommodator responds to this action as if being vomited on—wiping himself wherever it seems that the vomit has landed on him. I have seen structures where there has been this type of rising crescendo of feeling and expression and where the vomiting was a violent retching, without actually bringing anything up, that left the client sweating and exhausted. The positive accommodators reassure the client that they will never invade him and that they will only feed him when he wishes to be fed. They also assure him that they do not need to feed him and that his eating is not a measure of their value or worth—that is, if he eats, it is entirely for him and not for them. Some clients have been utterly taken over by negative parents, if not with their food then with their ideas, and these clients have a powerful wish to rid themselves of the invading ideas.

The various ways in which a client sucks on the positive mother have a striking relationship to how much he has expelled t he negative mother. If he has not fully expelled the negative mother, he may not suck with any force or feeling, and one can observe that he hardly takes any part of the flesh of the arm or hand of his positive accommodator into his mouth. Sometimes the so-called act of sucking is more a means of holding out the "nipple" with the teeth than an act of hungry and interested acceptance. After he has fully retched out or expelled the negative mother, he may take in the "nipple" with a loving passion. The same kind of sequence could occur regarding the expulsion of any negative energy followed by the interested intake of the positive.

When the client is happily sucking on the positive mother, it is important that the therapist find out the fantasy that is occurring. This should be done at such a time and in such a manner that it does not disturb the level of the feelings or break the rhythm of the action. The fantasy must be checked, for it is possible that the client is not thinking of the breast and nipple of the good mother at all, and may be feeling as if the hand of the accommodator is like a penis and experiencing the sucking sexually as if fellatio was being performed. I don't mean to say that the client finds that fantasy frightening or unpleasant; it might well be that when he thinks of a woman's breast in his mouth that he finds that thought unpleasant and can only suck with pleasure when it is a penis he has in mouth and mind. The therapist must then find some way to use the energy and satisfaction that is found in sucking the penis and transfer that to breast sucking if nurturance is what is needed. Perhaps the client could start by sucking, thinking that it was a penis, and then, with the same feeling, include the imagery of a breast.

Another tack would be to have the negative father, holding a rolled up newspaper or some other such symbolic object at his crotch, approach the client saying, "Here, you can get nurturance from sucking on my penis." The client may get angry at such an offer and reject the penis as a feeding organ. However, he may also feel, "Okay Dad, let me at it," and be perfectly willing to go along with the offer. If the client seems to be moving in that direction, it is preferable for the good father, holding a similar penis-like object at his crotch to say, "My penis does not give milk, I only put it into mother's vagina. I will never put it in your mouth." He might even make the gesture of pulling a symbolic cock out of the client's mouth. It is then possible that the client might feel the loss and be willing to go to the mother's breast as a substitute, accepting that as an alternative to nothing.

There are times when some clients wish actually to feel the milk or some fluid in their mouths when they do a nurturance structure. Some clients have brought baby bottles to the session so that their sucking on the good mother will produce something tangible. The use of a baby bottle has produced some interesting insights, for one client discovered that previous to the arrival of the bottle he enjoyed sucking on the good mother very much, but if he sucked on the good mother and used the baby bottle with actual milk, he found that he could not swallow the milk and that his fantasy was that the milk would taste awful or poison him. This brought out another level of trust or distrust of the good mother. He could be close to her, but he could not permit something from her body to enter him. It is also possible that further discrimination was needed between mother as a person and mother as food, for the milk could have seemed symbolically to have been the mother's blood and swallowing it would have been tantamount to eating mother herself. The milk could have been experienced as having a bad taste in order to inhibit the cannibalistic wish to consume mother, for the first mode of mouth relationship with mother can be verbalized as "relating is consuming." This type of relating can be seen in everyday reality with those people who seem literally to eat up a relationship, making it hard or impossible for those they wish to consume to relate to anyone else but them. They demand constant and total attention and if thwarted feel as if they are going to die, because they feel alive only if they have "eaten" people and relationships sufficiently. This type of behavior represents a great deficit of oral nurture and the energy that clients spend on interactions of this sort must be brought to bear on the structures where they are sucking on the good breast, to make sure that the sucking is not understood as consuming the mother. Yet there are times when a client wishes to feel as if he is literally taking the mother in so that he can feel complete. It seems worthwhile to permit temporary fantasizing on that level, for the reality experience is that the mother remains totally intact and in view, and what the client calls the experiencing of taking in or incorporating the mother may mean something else, and may be necessary for him to experience before he is ready for further discriminations.

Obviously the interactions and changes of feeling during a structure are subtle and swift, and the therapist must keep aware of them and permit and offer only those experiences that would lead toward maturation and growth. How does the therapist stop those experiences or structures that he feels would lead toward the reinforcement of negative expectations and behavior? He can interrupt the structure and point out that such and such a structure and accommodation would lead the client toward further behavior that was the very kind that he, the client, was trying to grow away from. If the client does not agree, then perhaps it is best to let him go on in whatever direction seems most satisfying to him, for he may have his own way of getting the kinds of things that would help him grow. However, if it seems over a period of time that the client is moving in a direction of pathology, the therapist must intervene and stop the process. This might lead to a showdown between the client and the therapist involving strong feelings on both sides as to what will or will not be allowable. The process of preventing the client from moving toward pathology might require a limiting structure, where the limits are placed on what seems to be the client's powerful wishes for negative nurturance and what might be called negative omnipotence. Negative omnipotence could be verbalized as, "Nobody is going to stop me from doing anything I want to do even if what I want is to hurt myself." In this case the limiting is being done both symbolically, with words, and in reality, with the leader and the client personally involved in the "now" interaction between them. It calls for the leader to be emotionally strong because he will be attacked on a personal level by the client, and even if it is understood to be only transference, the feelings that flow from the client to the therapist can be personally painful.

Kissing

One hospitalized client recounted how much she loved to kiss her boyfriends. The kissing would go on for long periods of time and never led to sex for she remained a virgin. When she demonstrated how she kissed her boyfriend by using her arms as her boyfriend, it seemed similar to how many other clients sucked on the good mother. One could conclude that in kissing she was substituting, or gratifying the need for nurturance on the infant level; however, it has seemed to me that it is impossible to gratify that oral need on the adult level by kissing. It seems easier and more effective to satisfy that oral deficit if one were to admit it and then satisfy it on the infant level with the appropriate target. The relationship this client had with boyfriends could be understood as a confusion of sexuality and nurturance and a fusion of her contemporary and her mother.

Kissing, if not used as a substitute for early oral deficits, becomes part of the tender, erotic mode of relationship that is satisfying in itself. Relating with the mouth is satisfying to the child, for that is how he survives and how he originally comprehends the world. When that level is grown out of, his mouth remains sensitive and is used to touch, caress and feel as well as speak. It not only functions to consume, but is used in an interpersonally relating mode. Placing one's mouth on the mouth of another represents high levels of trust and intimacy and caring and can be deeply satisfying.

Sometimes kissing is an important way for the expression of gratitude, for it often appears as a body impulse or wish at the end of a satisfying structure. The client, at the end of the structure, might be in the process of separating from his accommodators while still holding or touching them and looking into their eyes. He can be noted to have small movements about the mouth at those times, and he might spontaneously kiss his accommodators on the cheek. I have noted that some clients involuntarily thrust their lips forward and incline their heads toward their accommodators, and when I have said, "You look like you would like to kiss them," they have replied that indeed that was just on their minds but they felt hesitant about doing it for they didn't know whether it was appropriate or not to do so. When they have followed their impulse and kissed their accommodators, it has seemed to satisfy some need or feeling, for then they exhale with that quality that indicates to me that a structure is over.

Let me elaborate on that exhalation. One of the aims of a structure is to reach the point of satiation or gratification that permits the transition from one mode to another. The exhalation has the quality that could be verbalized as "That's good, I feel finished, complete and ready to go on to something else or to rest." It is the kind of feeling one has at the end of any good experience, whether it be a meal, sex, a good performance, the end of a job well done, the end of a party when the last guest has gone, and so forth. That kind of exhalation and concomitant body relaxation seems to be a rhythmic marker that indicates the end of a process. A structure is never entirely over until such a feeling is experienced and expressed. I have never verbalized this in my groups, for it might lead some clients to make that sound because they know it represents the end of a satisfying structure and they wish to have satisfying structures or wish to please me by having satisfying structures. But that change of breathing is always present at the end of a structure and if it has not shown even though a client might say that he is finished, I may superficially agree and behave as if the structure is over, but leave opportunities open for the client to continue the structure. Sometimes the client might not pick up those opportunities and might not finish that structure until some future time. Of course it is not possible always to finish with total satisfaction, particularly when one is working in a weekly group with only twenty-five minutes available for a structure. However, in a weekend workshop the time is longer and more flexible, and this transitional level can be reached.

The relaxation that is associated with the exhalation seems to me to be rhythmic and transitional. It marks the end of a totality and indicates a shift of experience and perspective and a readiness, perhaps following some rest, to enter something new or some new experience with fresh energy and viewpoint. Life is dynamic and seeks interaction, each interaction having its own gestalt and capacity for completion. The falling, relaxing rhythm at the end of such a gestalt should not be misunderstood as the goal and total aim of the energy expression that preceded it.

It is only with such satisfying experiences that one is capable of moving up the developmental scale. The end of one series or set of experiences seems to mark some physiological or neurological boundary that permits the next stage or set of experiences to be entered. Just as the example of the client who was not finished until she had kissed her accommodators indicates, there is a nagging suspension of closure while certain sets of impulses or satisfactions remain unexperienced or unexpressed. I believe that we as people carry about unsatisfied sets of needs from our childhood that nag at us and seek expression in indirect ways until we pay sufficient attention to them to close out their accounts via the route of pleasure and satisfaction. Certainly the capacity to postpone pleasure is indicative of maturity and is necessary for adult life, but even as adults we must experience our measure of pleasure or life loses its lustre and value. As children or infants we must satisfy all of our basic needs or we might not make it through the first years.

Psychomotor therapy seems to provide an arena for the settling of unfinished accounts. All records are kept and the books are never closed until we die. Even if we are fifty the record of unfinished business is still available and can be settled by the satisfying doing of structures. Then that fifty-year-old can be rid of forty-nine-year-old past due bills and use all of his energy to be fifty years old with satisfaction.

Another Rhythmic Marker

The group leader can recognize when a client has completed the negative or fearful aspects of his structure by noting certain changes in the client's breathing and more particularly in his digestive sounds. The change in breathing might make both the client and the therapist believe that the structure was over, but although it is quieter than the excited breathing of the angry expressions in the negative part of the structure, it is not as quiet as the settled, finished breathing discussed above. With the change in breathing comes, frequently, the sound of gurglings in the stomach or even a burp. This marks an ending of fear and anger and a readiness for the positive input. It is as if the therapist were hearing the external manifestations of the switch from the sympathetic to the parasympathetic nervous systems.

When the rhythm has changed, it is wise to work with those new issues that the client would more likely respond to rather than to bring back issues that he has temporarily left and which his nervous system is no longer geared toward. The therapist must deal with what he has in front of him and must not ignore the mood and feelings of his client, for when he follows the flow of the client's rhythm and emotions, the client knows and feels that it is his own structure and not imposed on him from without by the therapist. The matching of feeling, behavior and accommodation is then congruent and satisfying and permits the client to grow and to leave old levels of feeling and behavior. If the client has not moved toward the stage of satisfaction and positive input, the therapist must help the client find those issues and forms of expression that might be keeping him from relaxing and going on to something new. At those times a scanning of the body might show areas of tension or small action which often can point the way to what is disturbing the client. One of those small areas, for example, could have been the mouth movements of the client discussed above, who wished to kiss the accommodators. Another area of tension might appear as some small movement around the mouth and forehead of the client that would indicate that he was formulating some words or thoughts he wished to express about the figures in the structures, and he should be encouraged to express them.

When a client is about to speak in a structure, the therapist can usually note that there is some kind of preparatory behavior preceding and predicting that fact. Sometimes the lips may begin to extend as if they are about to speak, or sometimes the tongue may pass over the lips, moistening them. Sometimes the client will take in his breath suddenly and hold it in for an instant preparatory to letting it out again while speaking. Sometimes the client might exhibit a fleeting frown and narrowing of the eyes while staring in front of himself as he collects his thoughts. All of this might be fairly overt and conscious, or some of it might be quite subtle and unconscious. There are times when a client might wish to say something about himself or his circumstances which is very meaningful, which might cause him pain or embarrassment and which must be dealt with before he can go on to anything else. If the therapist has missed the clues telling him what is potentially happening, he might find the client either doing nothing or moving in his structure without real feeling. It is best to wait out the hesitations to speak at this point and to be helpful and patient until the words and feelings spill out and then the rhythm of expression can be met and maintained.

Smiling

A smile is indicative of pleasure, and since pleasure is one of the goals of a structure, a smile is useful as a gauge of congruency between behavior and accommodation. The smile can be a result of satisfying accommodation to anger and not only the result of direct pleasurable satisfaction such as one might gain out of a nursing structure. That is, when the negative figure reacts with pain or loss of balance to the blows of the client, the client might smile instead of showing anger on his face. Of course the client does not continue smiling while he goes through the rest of his anger. He may have a wide range of expressions on his face as he expresses his anger. The smile that occurs when anger is being expressed usually occurs at the very outset. The situation might be as follows: the client may be in a weekend workshop and have never yet gone through a structure. He may have some feelings in his hands or in some part of his body which indicate anger. If the accommodator offers a wide range of responses to the movement of the client, the client might not react at all until the accommodator responds as if bitten, hit, or somehow attacked by the client, and then the client might smile. The smile would indicate that a "match" had been achieved and that we were on the right track. Of course the smile could be a result of something completely unassociated with anger. For instance, a client might say that he felt like his knees were buckling and that he wanted to fall to the floor. When told that good parents might be available to give him support, he might smile and say, "That would be good," indicating an appropriate match.

Sometimes a client might smile as described above and then say, "But I don't feel angry," or whatever emotion had been ascribed to him. If it were pointed out to him that he seemed to like the kind of accommodation he was receiving, he might say that he just thought the actions of his accommodator were funny or ludicrous and that is what made him react the way he did. It does not do well to push the point, for in any case the client is not experiencing what it might appear that he was. For even if the therapist was correct in his interpretation of the client's bodily responses, the client's verbal-symbolic ego was not accepting these bodily responses as his own, indicating a distance between the body and symbolic egos. Anger or whatever emotions were being exhibited might not be a permissible word or concept to the client and therefore not real or available for experience.

This kind of knowledge has led my recent work with groups toward a more conscious effort to knit together the body ego and the symbolic ego. In the past I have seen many clients go through fantastic expressions of emotion which followed directly out of the motoric impulses and which were predictable from all the tensions and actions that were showing up on the body. Yet those clients sometimes had some difficulty making any kind of sense out of their behavior even though the therapist and the rest of the group were perfectly aware of what the issues were. That person's individual and personal system of symbols did not have sufficient words or concepts to deal with what he found himself doing, and it often took weeks of talking to pull together all the material that was expressed in a single structure. If that person had no opportunity to discuss therapy and had only a single weekend experience in psychomotor therapy, it is entirely probable that little if any of the emotional material was integrated into conscious awareness and therefore available for growth and learning.

The body ego and motoric behavior is much more concrete, clear and predictable than the verbal ego. The interpersonal, interactive motoric behaviors conform to seeming stereotypical norms built into our nervous systems, but the flexibility and variety of the verbal-symbolic systems seem to permit tremendous variety and individuality of thoughts and ideas. It seems fairly impossible to be able to predict what goes on in the mind from anything that shows on the outside, whereas one can fairly accurately predict what is going on emotionally and motorically from what shows up in body tensions. The important point is that those tensions may have different symbols and meanings for each individual who experiences it. Those differences are what make therapy continually exciting and new. Now, instead of simply *facilitating* the emotional expression of a tension motorically, I take time to find what it means symbolically and verbally to the client ally. In that way the conscious ego of the client is always available and working, and the experience is not permitted to slip ble and working, and the experience is not permitted to slip by and simply be tucked away as a happening or a "trip." The total process seems to be one of "being yourself" in your body and maturing the body ego while accepting that being consciously and having the verbal ego become more congruent with what is felt and how that feeling is being expressed.

Hand to Mouth in Reflection

I have previously noted the relationship between metabolic functioning and thinking. There is a hand gesture of placing the fingers on the mouth and the mouth may even be making small biting or sucking movements. This gesture is not so indicative of a nurturant need as it is an indication that the client is reflecting or mentally "metabolizing," so to speak. Of course, there may be times when the client who is asked to report what he is thinking at those times might reply that he was thinking of food, but there is a type of hand-to-mouth gesture that is truly not nurturant and more indicative of the mental set of reflection. How does one discriminate between the nurturant gesture and the reflective gesture? Perhaps it is in the level of sensuous involvement. There are those times when it seems perfectly clear that the gesture is satisfying a strictly oral need because of the emotional involvement and intensity of the movement. There is also the factor of the eye focus at those reflective moments which may indicate that the client is thinking and not concerned or involved particularly with the sensation of his hand on his mouth.

Feelings in the Throat

When a person complained that he feels a lump in the throat, it has often meant to me that he feels like crying, and experience often confirms it. Sometimes people in groups say they are trying to swallow down the feeling but they can be encouraged to give way to the desire to cry rather than to suppress it. When some clients cry after expressing this sensation of a lump in the throat, they may weep soundlessly; however, this does not thoroughly express the need to cry and does not result in the throat feeling normal. There is a need to cry with sounds coming from the throat. Of course one does not force one's self to make those sounds, but rather one permits those sounds to be expressed. Sometimes when a client does begin to cry fully and freely, the pain of the crying becomes almost unbearable and the client may say that he cannot bear the anguish that he is feeling. I have encouraged such clients to continue their expression, and tell them that the pain will not kill them or burst them apart even if it feels as if it might. It seems as if one must fully experience an emotion even before it can be integrated or grown out of. Sometimes an event is accompanied by pain and the fear of the pain. Before the event can be assimilated the pain must be experienced and lived through. The lump can be described as a physical representation of the energy that must be processed at the throat. However, I must add that the extreme forms of pain and grief are not experienced simply as lumps in the throat. It is the tight feeling in the chest around the sternum that bespeaks a deep grief and need to cry that is harder to process. When a client is going through the grief experience, his breathing almost becomes choked off and the crying results in a feeling of a collapsed or an exploded chest. One client in the throes of that expression almost seemed willing to leave his body to avoid the crushing sensation, saying, "I can't stand it, I can't stand it." He was helped through the feelings, and it was found that they related to the loss of his mother at an early age and that he had never permitted himself to feel fully his emotional reaction to that loss. Following several intense sessions of expressing his grief and feelings of total loss of life, he turned an experiential corner and became more adult in a realistic and not omnipotent way, and his actual facial expressions and body sense changed in that he seemed less fragile and more "present" in his body. It seemed as if his body literally "filled out"—not that he gained weight, he didn't, but he looked more physically substantial. This situation did not arise immediately, for this client was in a group for a year before this sequence occurred.

Other feelings in the throat can indicate the need or wish to scream or shout. The screams can be in fear, rage, frustration or indignation. Whenever those feelings are permitted full and complete expression, it is startling to either the group or the client how real the emotions are. When I have permitted myself to respond to such throat feelings that indicated a wish to shout, I have found myself in the position of being a surprised onlooker to a portion of myself that is real and experiencing that feeling and yet just previously was separate from conscious awareness of it. After the first shout or cry, which is an exact replica of a child-like cry or deep sob of emotion from some previous experience of mine, perhaps long forgotten, I can explore once again and permit myself to express the feeling and see what sounds and other feelings result. It may be anguish, childish crying for help, or adult rage, and the feelings flow and with the flow comes ideation and memories that a short period of talk or reflection organizes into a meaningful whole. It has been my experience that the talk should not come too soon or in place of the expression, for then the full memory and symbolic attachments will not be forthcoming. When the process is complete and the verbal integration added to it, it becomes impossible to make those sounds again. Not because of muscle strictures or being tired, but because those complex sets of feelings and muscle tensions are no longer available to produce those very specific sounds. I am not saying that one never again can make those sounds; one simply has to feel the same emotions again, but it is impossible to "imitate" those sounds without it being apparent to one's self and to others that it is an imitation.

It can be an uncanny feeling to have such sounds come out of one's self, sounds so seemingly total and yet so unknown to one's self that it calls for much work to find a place for such feelings in one's understanding of one's self. Some clients have become puzzled at hearing those noises coming from their own throats; however, they should not be allowed to dismiss them as strange, unrelated fragments of emotion which have little or nothing to do with their "real" selves. It is possible that such clients have had lives that to others would be unbearably stifling but which they have borne with quiet resignation on the surface because they considered that this was all that life had to offer and all that they deserved. Those clients have to be led to a place where their organic or emotional rebellion against such treatment can be recognized and accepted by themselves.

Sometimes the feeling in the throat can be as if something is stuck there. At first it might feel as if something palpable were stuck there and then it often becomes an idea or feeling or expression that is stuck there. For instance, it might be an unwillingness to "swallow" some feeling or expression imposed on one by others, or the unexpressed wish to tell someone off. It might also be a wish to have something in the throat such as food or nurturance of some kind, and the client might have an ambivalent desire both to swallowing it in order to be fed and therefore to be able to live, and not to swallow it because the symbolic form of the nurturance might be sexual, for example a penis, and he might unconsciously be shocked at the thought of such "food."

Obviously the therapist must not leap to conclusions regarding the origin of the feeling. He must permit the client the widest latitude of expression and ideation and help the client find what is actually going on inside himself.

Feelings in the Neck

The feeling of stiffness in the neck is associated most frequently with control and inhibition. There is no way to tell what the inhibition is about, for the neck tension does not specifically indicate any other body part. My tendency is to regard the stiff neck as an unconscious attempt to keep the feelings from going into the rest of the body. That is, I imagine it to be as if there was some process going on whereby the feelings were squeezed off at the neck and not permitted to reach the body. Frequently, those people who complain of stiff necks at the outset of a structure can go right on to have a satisfactory and satisfying expression of feelings motorically, so stiff necks do not indicate the capacity for motoric expression, but point to inhibition and restraint.

Sometimes when a client speaks of tight feelings in the neck he may mean the trapezius muscles descending from the neck to the shoulders. That is why I ask clients to point to the place when they are having the feeling. Those muscles come into play when the shoulders are raised and can indicate a wish to hide or be protected—to pull the head into the shoulders and protect the vulnerable neck.

Feelings in the Shoulder

Feelings in the shoulders most frequently lead to use of the arms, for the shoulders cannot make much movement of their own save to raise in protection. When a client notes shoulder tension and then attempts to motorically free-associate to see what movement occurs or suggests itself, some specific memories concerning that part of the body usually arise. It might be that at one time he was hit upon the shoulder in an argument, or he may have been thrown from a car and landed on that shoulder. Sometimes it leads to associations about having something on his back like a weight which is pressing down on him. This may develop into a structure about having responsibility burdens placed too soon upon him, or a structure about concerns and responsibilities that he is straining under at that time.

Very often shoulder stiffness leads toward feelings of anger which provide strong movements of the arms. This is a bit of a puzzle to me, for the most frequent expression of a tension that points to anger is in the upper arm and forearm. For some people the tension does not seem to get that far and settles in the shoulders.

It is possible that the feeling in the shoulders might indicate a wish to be touched in that area as well as a wish to move the body in that area. The shoulders are an important place for receiving comfort and protection, and it is possible that the client might want to feel an arm or a hand on his shoulder in sympathy, encouragement, support or protection. The therapist might suggest to the client to see how it feels to have someone touch him where he feels the tension and then to note or monitor his reaction to it.

Feelings in the Upper Back

There is not much to say about the area of the upper back except that pains or tensions felt there most frequently lead toward strong arm movement such as is found in expression of anger. Once again I must note that the area of tension is some distance from the arms and could represent an attempt to repress the feeling.

Feelings in the Arms

The arms are the most common area for feelings of anger. Most clients when associating emotions with tension in the arms arrive most readily at the idea of anger. An attempt to express the anger using the arms is usually sufficient to pull up the rest of the feelings. But the arms are instruments of highly varied behavior, and it is possible that the tension might lead to many other actions. For instance, it could be that the client wished to hit, but there might be an element of poking involved in it which in the sense of penetrating could have many different kinds of connotations, including sexual. The tension might reflect curiosity and a wish to look inside some object in the room. It could also be a wish to push or keep something away from one's self and might make the client want to hold his arms stiff. Sometimes it has resulted in swimming-type movements reflecting an early experience in the water.

One hospitalized client had for the longest time a feeling that his arms were pulling out of their sockets as if they were going to pull themselves right off at the shoulders. I interpreted this as a guilt reaction to tremendously strong angry feelings which I knew that this patient had.

The arms can also express warm feelings, and tension felt there can precede a movement to embrace someone. At the first those clients might even be seen embracing themselves as they explore what their arms wish to do. The therapist can suggest to them that there may be someone outside themselves whom they can hug, and this can lead to a structure regarding their willingness to hug others or their feelings of worthiness or unworthiness as the recipient of warm feelings from others.

When a client uses his arms in an angry fashion after finding an arm tension that seems to be an expression of imminent anger, one would expect that the arm tension would reduce and yet there are times when this is not the result. The client might punch and scream for long periods of time without feeling any lessening of either the tension or the anger. This leads me to suggest to the client that there is more emotion available than he is presently able to process and that perhaps he would benefit from a limiting structure (where the group holds him on the mat as extensions of the good parents who say that no matter how angry he gets they are not going to permit him to kill anyone or himself). When the group holds that client, it is possible that even more energetic movement is produced than when he was able to move in an unrestrained fashion, and the group has to work hard physically to restrain him. If this is the appropriate structure, the client will report that he feels no more tension in his arms and is relieved that there is someone stronger than he is who can control him.

Watching a client's arms during the course of a structure can be instructive and can keep a therapist aware of the level of energy with which the client is working. If the arms fall to the side and the hands are slack, it can sometimes mean depression and hopelessness as well as relaxation, depending on the rest of the cues the client presents. Arms held away from the body seem to represent readiness for action or tension and an attitude of alert and possibly defensive aware-ness. When the arms drop from that position, one can be pretty certain that it represents a change to another emotional state, whether it be security or defeat. Many chronic men-tal patients whom I observed during research on a test at the Boston Veteran's hospital never let their arms drop. It could bespeak a constant tension and readiness for defense.

The arms are sometimes used symbolically by both males and females as a phallus. This is done both consciously and unconsciously. An upraised arm with the hand fisted can represent both aggressive power and sexual potency. I remember a gesture we used as children in Brooklyn that was a non-verbal equivalent of "fuck you." The right arm was thrust upward with the hand fisted, the arm bent at the elbow while simultaneously the left hand was kind of slap-pressed against the right bicep at the elbow. The left hand was open and was pressing against and restraining the for-ward and upward motion of the right arm as if the right forearm was being thrust up to the hilt only coming to a stop by coming in contact with the pubic-bone-palm of the left hand. The gesture was sometimes accompanied by a kind of kissing sound made by the mouth which in retrospect sounds like the appropriate squishing noise that would be made by a plunging phallus.

There is a gesture in vogue nowadays amongst the rebeling young that is similar to the one described except that it is not as obviously aggressive in that the fist is incomplete due to the extension of the middle finger upward and the left hand is not used in a restraining up-to-the-hilt-suggesting action. The verbal equivalent in this case is "up yours" and suggests not so much sexuality as a violation and invasion of the self. To me it includes a penetration of the ego or protective skin-membrane of the self, not so much sexual as a denial or the integrity and intactness of the object.

Another gesture that is made consciously by many males but which shows up unconsciously in some females during a structure is one that suggests the words "screw you." The fisted forearm is thrust horizontally forward while the forearm rotates making a kind of screwing motion. This can show up in any number of points in a structure; in a male who is speaking of his mother toward whom he has conscious or unconscious sexual desires; in a female who is directing that action toward her father in an unconscious wish to ward off father's overt sexual attentions by growing a screwing penis of her own in defense; in an angry female who would like to get back at her husband who is treating her harshly as an aggressive sexual object without concomitant love and tenderness.

A client can be using his arms as a protective shield when in outward appearance it looks as if he is hugging himself. In this case it is not the intention to give warmth to the self but to protect the self from outside stimulus. The arms in this case are holding the world out. This is similar to the gesture of placing the hands over the ears to hold sounds out, but in this case actions toward the self are being kept out.

The Hand

Besides the face, hands are the most expressive parts of human beings. Hands are constantly changing, emphasizing, accenting and explicitly stating what is being felt and expressed in either verbal or non-verbal communication. An entire volume could be written on the subject; hence I will only skim over the major items as I have done previously with the other parts of the body. Hands not only are expressive but are an important part of sensory imput through touch. We know the world most personally by our sense of touch, by feeling the world with our hands. Certainly we have a sense of touch everywhere on our bodies, but nowhere except the mouth is it sensitive and as manipulable as with the hands. Animals "handle" most objects with their mouths, whereas humans handle them with their hands.

Knowing by feeling or by touch is very personal and close to our actual motoric, muscular, concrete selves. Smelling, hearing and seeing are all distance perceptions whereas we touch the world with ourselves, as evidenced by the statement when we are deeply moved, "that was touching."

The hands are involved in sensing and therefore are partly an ego perception function. They are also used in the process of standing, or at least as assistants in the process of learning to stand and are used in the reflexive body as righting mechanisms to throw our center of gravity over our feet or, in the event that fails, to grasp for objects of support or to cushion the impact of the falling body. Following the fall hands are used to lug us back to a standing position. Hands are important in the metabolic or eating arena, obviously to grasp food and bring it to the mouth. For the infant, hands are used to clutch the mother and to hang on as a primate infant can hang on to the mother while she swings through the branches; and, too, the baby's hands can be seen reflexively squeezing the breast as it nurses. The hand, then, is important to the stomach.

The hand is used in many interpersonally interactive ways and is the means of first social contact through the handshake. The handshake is no mere ritual; it gives us a feel of the other fellow. Is he warm or cold, is he wet or dry, is he weak or strong, does he hold on for a long or short time, is he steady or uneven? The hand can bring someone close to us or push them away. The hand can slap or punch or penetrate.

The hand is the prime manipulator of things. The hand takes things apart, puts them together, destroys and builds. The hand weighs objects and measures their relative span. Hands can discriminate shapes in a different way than the eyes do because they can assume so many different shapes themselves—a straight line is a flat palm, a circle is a thumb and forefinger curved to touch each other, a hemisphere is a cupped hand, and so forth. Obviously the hands can move in abstract ways and are used for symbolic expression as with the sign language of the deaf.

The hands, then, work within the range of interactive energy systems as well as participating in ego functions. The hand, like the mouth, can be understood to represent the entire self. This is not to say that the self "resides" in the hand, but that the hand in ordinary living can be expressive of the self as it has from the earliest years been an active participant in the being of the self. Consider, however, the case of the Irish novelist who has only the control of the toes of one foot, with which he types out his works. Certainly, he is an example of a creative self who does not need the use of hands for the expression of his artistry and being. The human self, then, uses whatever sources are at its disposal for its expression, its essential selfness residing perhaps in the brain and spirit of the person and in no particular bodily spot. This is an important issue and one with which I hope to close the book at the end of this chapter. The essential question is, "Where does the essential self reside in the human and what part does bodily expression have in it?"

To return to the hands, during a structure I watch the face and hands of the client, as well as note other areas of the body which seem energized and activated, to monitor the entire range of possibilities of expression inherent in the hands and to try to correlate that data with whatever else the client is doing and saying. This is a tall order and I cannot suggest that I do it thoroughly, but it is something I make conscious and intuitive attempts to understand. There seem to be times when the hands emphasize and accent what is being said and done and times when the hands seem to be irrelevant or indifferent to what is being said and done. How is one to make sense of all those possibilities? My solution has been to construct consciously, unconsciously and intuitively a rapid series of scenarios or gestalts which might predict an outcome, direction or structure that would unify or make sense out of the data that is being demonstrated and what I have learned about the client from previous sessions. After a while one may become proficient in organizing the data surrounding a particular client into some standard scenarios within which he can be better understood. Or one may become adept in convincing a client that he is indeed feeling what one thinks he is feeling but that limits, if not prevents, the discovery of what is represented by the speech and actions of the client. There are times when the art of watching and listening feels no more accurate or scientific than tea leaf reading or studying the entrails of sacrificial animals. Putting all such discouragements aside, there are also times when clients become practiced in listening to and watching themselves and lead themselves step by step to an understanding of what their words and actions mean.

Hands will sometimes fall open in a requesting gesture during nurturance with the good mother, and it becomes clear that it is not only the mouth which must be attended to, but the hand also. When the accommodators see a client's hand make such a gesture, they may either clasp it to conform to its shape or make their hands into giving shapes and place their fingers into the outstretched requesting hand. The hand may in similar circumstances also be seeking the firm, strong hand of the father to experience his strength while receiving warmth and love from the mother orally. The hand in that same circumstance might be held tentatively off the back of the good mother as if it cannot come to rest comfortably on her and as if it is about to be used to push someone off at any moment. The hand might be squeezing the back of the mother in rhythmic pulses as the client sucks on the "breast" of the good mother, much as infants squeeze the breast of the mother in the actual nursing experience. The hands may be holding the good mother so tightly that the accommodator might experience sharp pains indicating that more than the idea of nurturance is in the client's mind. It is possible in that event that the client is experiencing anger in conjunction with the nurturance and needs to have a way to express it more directly. The anger can be directed at the negative mother which then permits or may permit the client to relax more thoroughly with the positive mother, who can respond with the statement that no matter how angry the child gets she can handle that child's feelings and still not deny that child its love and nurturance.

Sometimes the hand may clutch at the clothes of the accommodators, indicating the possibility of fear of loss or abandonment by the parents. The good parents can respond to this by saying that they will not abandon the client. This perhaps might produce a memory of actual abandonment which can then be dealt with in the structure. Sometimes a client might be seen stroking himself while he is in a structure and this can lead to an inquiry as to whether he would like someone other than himself to stroke him or whether he is directing toward himself a tenderness that he wishes to but does not dare place on some other.

There is a hospitalized patient whom I see whose hands are constantly relating to one another with intensity and apparent feeling but which go dead the moment they touch someone else. It is clear that this person is unwilling and unable to place feelings via the hands on anyone but himself. In this case the fingernails of one hand can be seen digging into the flesh and skin of the other hand and one can almost imagine seeing interactive energy flowing across from one hand to another which should be placed on outside people.

Often, those clients who are experiencing guilt about their angry feelings will be seen pounding one fist into the palm of another when a nearby pillow or mattress would take the impact better than themselves. Those clients say that it feels better and possibly more relieving when they hurt themselves than when they direct their anger at others.

Sometimes a client can be talking preparatory to doing a structure and his hands can be seen picking pieces of dust off himself and throwing them away or brushing invisible specks off his clothes. This could be interpreted as a grooming mechanism or could be seen as an attempt or wish to be rid of something, possibly dirty, that is on one's self. Clients in those circumstances sometimes report that they wish to throw away bad feelings rather than feel them and identify them as legitimate parts of themselves. This can also be understood as a wish to throw themselves away, too.

Sometimes hands are clasped in a gesture of contentment and self-repose. At other times the hands are clasped tightly and with self-control, holding feelings in and feelings out. Sometimes a hand might show that peculiar gesture of the fingers being crossed. This can happen in a support or nurturance structure and some experiences have shown that the client has been holding on to himself and not daring to trust others or invest himself completely. This is not done intentionally, but more often looks like the middle finger is lightly rubbing or "interested" in the nail of the index finger. In a way it is sort of magical gesture which protects one from possible pain in an emotional investment by pretending "I really didn't mean it; I had my fingers crossed all the time."

Another magical use of the hands is demonstrated by a hospitalized client of mine who shows her love for others by knocking on wood in sets of threes in order to protect her friends from evil or hurt. There are also many kinds of religious and magical gestures, too numerous to mention, that have come down through time which have protection value. Whenever I see a client make a gesture which I have not seen before, I question him about it to see if it is done consciously and within the context of his religious symbol system. Sometimes the gesture might have been done unconsciously, and when it is brought to his attention it brings back long-forgotten but suddenly vivid memories of religious experiences that somehow are pertinent to the present set of feelings and circumstances.

One female client suddenly began to scratch vigorously at the fleshy base of her thumb while talking about her mother. Thumbs are often used phallically in structures, and it seemed to me that this client had sexual feelings of a masculine or phallic nature toward her mother. In this particular case I mentioned this to the client (she had already let it be known that she had homosexual feelings toward women) so that her relationship to her good mother would be more clearly nurturant and minimally sexual. She grew annoyed with me for my interpretation but said with a smile on her face, "Can't I just scratch my thumb because it is itchy?" Then, as she resumed talking, the middle finger of the hand she was scratching bent upward in the classic position of digital vaginal entry, an action and position of which she was not conscious and which she had not heretofore demonstrated. Of course she could have been "putting me on," but I do not think so for her hands were fairly relaxed in her lap except for that middle finger.

There seems to be a series of gestures which naturally follow sexual feelings and thoughts in some people, and I would like to enumerate a few. Some clients seem to have finger intercourse, one hand with the other, for one or sometimes two fingers can be observed rhythmically and sensually pushing into the partially closed opposite hand while the client is talking. The significance of this is highly varied depending on whether the client is male or female and what the client happens to be talking about and to whom at that moment. The point is that the significance has to do with each individual moment and is not to be understood as a blanket assessment of that patient's state of mind for all time.

Other female clients sometimes stand while holding in one hand two fingers, the middle and the index, of the other hand for long periods of time without moving. This seems to suggest to me that there is a support need or a need to hold onto themselves instead of having someone else to hold onto. My conjecture includes the possibility that it is daddy's penis that they are holding onto as a symbol of his manliness and capacity to protect them. The penis in this event would have more meaning as a symbol of strength than as a sexual symbol.

Sometimes clients both male and female will point their index fingers at each other and bounce the tips of these fingers together lightly while all the other fingers are curled under. This has suggested to me that those clients are experiencing a kind of homosexual wish or relationship with the father, whether they be male or female. That is, they seem to be wishing a penis-to-penis relationship, with the father seen as peer or equal and with an undercurrent of sexual relationship with neither of them playing the female. Of course this can be simply a figment of my own imagination, but that frame of reference has often seemed valid in understanding certain client's relationships with their fathers.

The very same clients described above also can be seen to make a gesture or shape their hands in their laps as if they are making the shape of a vagina. At those particular moments those clients, when asked to verbally associate, frequently are experiencing a wish to be receptive.

Monitoring hand gestures sometimes offers fascinating clues to otherwise confusing and contradictory expressions. I find that if I trust the motoric statements, even without openly or directly interpreting them, I can keep in touch with the essential material and meaning of a structure and help the client realize his other levels of meaning. This is a subtle and peculiar business and one can easily, as I often have, be led astray by one's own excited imagination especially if the client is willing to play along with all kinds of interpretations for want of anything else that makes sense to him about his psyche. But that is not the way to growth and maturity. It is best to play down the spectacular and creative insights until one is quite sure that what one thinks he has seen can be believed. And even then the meanings are anything but certain.

The point of all the information gathering should be to assist the client to integrate motorically and emotionally and cognitively all that he is, so that those expressions that are covert and symbolic and which should be part of his active behavior can gain the energy that has been shunted off into other areas. That behavior can then be developed and helped to gain the appropriate targets and ends.

Feelings in the Stomach

Feelings in the stomach naturally have much to do with the needs of eating and eliminating, that is, the metabolic system, but they can also refer to the procreative process. This makes sense, for often eating and becoming pregnant, eliminating and giving birth, can be associated or confused with one another.

Pains in the stomach can also be associated with general tension and anxiety that is not strictly associated with either eating or sexuality. Some emotions can "upset the stomach" just as if they were kinds of food, and the body responds as if it is having emotional indigestion. Those emotions, when either processed and integrated or catharted in the sense of being eliminated, no longer make the stomach feel queasy; that is, the pains go away when the feelings are dealt with. If angry feelings are upsetting the stomach, one can understand the difficulty that the stomach is having, for how does a stomach act angry? The chemicals and nervous stimulation that would produce angry behavior in the skeletal muscles, behavior such as punching and hitting, has little or no way to be processed in the stomach. When that energy is permitted the normal expression in the normal channels, the stomach accumulation of energy and tension is processed muscularly and effectively, and the distress is no longer experienced.

Clients complaining of pains or uncomfortable feelings in the stomach often begin to recall feeding and eliminating problems which they experienced during childhood. Some mothers force their children to eat everything on their plate before leaving the table, and sometimes the pain is associated with that. Other times clients recall endless enemas of their childhood and remember with pain and discomfort the distended stomach feeling while they held the water in as they headed, for the bathroom. Some clients associate the full, distended stomach with being pregnant, and fantasies about a baby coming out of their anus ensue. Obviously, some clients have difficulty eating because they may fantasize that eating would make them pregnant. The pregnancy associations are so complex that it is impossible to do justice to all of them, but it is not infrequent that the real identity of the client's self is tied up with the ideas of the infant they imagine they are carrying. I have observed in many structures the combination of expressions that occur around the straining to eliminate, the straining to give birth and the straining to have feelings come out. Sometimes all these actions and feelings are going on simultaneously. It is as if they are indeed giving birth or experiencing the labor of giving birth, but it is themselves that they end up giving birth to!

When a child feels that his mother pays most attention to him by the consistent giving of enemas, it might seem to the child that the anus is more important than the mouth as a receptor for nurturance. The primary mode of relating and emotional interacting then revolves around the feelings of being penetrated and ministered to anally. The confusions about this are obvious, and the structures attempt to sort out the feelings and behaviors, with the good mother saying, "I do not feed you through your anus, I feed you by giving you good milk from my breast to your mouth. I do not feed you with an enema tube and I will not penetrate you or be interested in you sexually." It is not all that simple, for no doubt the client has developed some sexual feelings associated with the enemas either consciously or unconsciously, and those feelings must be permitted to surface and then be shunted or utilized in direct sexual expression.

Surprisingly, the feelings about the anus are among the most repressed feelings that are dealt with in psychomotor therapy. Most people have little shame discussing most sexual matters these days, but the anus connected with sex or anything pleasurable seems fairly taboo. The mouth is attended to and understood, and the genitals, too, but the anus is the site of dirty feelings. Perhaps this is why sex—dirty sex, that is—is called smut, because somewhere it still has anal attachments and associations and the anus is where the really dirty stuff is.

Pains in the stomach can also be associated with feelings of hunger and deprivation; however, the means of satisfying those feelings can be a combination of sex and nurturance and the problem of the structure is to help sort out those feelings with the appropriate figures.

The issue of toilet training is strongly involved with stomach feelings. Around this issue develop many concepts about productivity connected with approval and love, invasion of the self and the attempts to keep intact in the face of such invasions. Invasion in the sense that the parent who toilet trains the child forcefully is experienced as violating the integrity of the self when he or she demands that something within the self is to be expelled on command. Resistance, stubbornness and holding on become intensified in such encounters, for that is the only defense that the child has for maintaining his wholeness and integrity. Unfortunately, these traits may have long lasting tenacity and be manifested long after such self-threatening situations have passed and the child has become an adult. This type of situation is often reflected in clients whose body reports include lower back pain.

Lower Back Pain

Experience has led me to associate lower back pain with stubborness and passive aggression. For whatever reason, those clients who consistently report lower back pain seem to have a conscious or unconscious wish to defecate on the world. Perhaps it is because their parents invaded them and made them defecate on command, perhaps it had nothing to do with toilet training but had to do with other types of invasion of the self, but a vengeful and forceful wish to aim the anal cannon at the target, press down on the gut and the lower back and let fly, often surfaces in such clients. It sometimes seems to me that those clients can get nowhere in structures or in a motoric type of therapy until they let that wish and behavior surface with the appropriate accomodation of the entire group wiping themselves. For if those clients do not overtly express such behavior they defecate on the group symbolically and indirectly instead. Nothing the group does or the therapist does can affect them. They make the group fail, make the therapist fail and make themselves fail.

However, if they can find some way to let their anger go in a vengeful and aggressive way, they turn from sad, down-in-the-mouth creatures to laughing, squatting imps who delight in the discomfort of the accommodators as they defecate in the accommodators' faces and see them drown in it. When those clients express the anger on a skeletal muscle level, it leaves the arena or organ expression which cannot properly handle that emotion.

When such a client first talks of lower back pain and then when it comes to his turn, which is usually toward the very end of the session, I have built up a set of negative expectations. Often I am "sucked in" by my wish to help, and I become easy meat for a passive aggressive who will arouse my sympathy with his problems and then prevent me from helping by thwarting all my attempts to reach him. I will, in a testing fashion, sometimes put out a feeler and say after a few attempts, "Gee, I am stumped, I don't know what to do to help you." If the client, who might previously have looked glum and disconsolate, perks up and smiles at such a statement, I know with whom I am dealing.

Sometimes clients will deny that they take pleasure in thwarting and will discount the smile on their faces by saying that it seemed like a silly remark and that is why they smiled. But one can note that even as they are saying that they often are in a squatting position or are on their knees leaning forward.

Sometimes a passive aggressive client will thwart the group to such a degree that the group then attempts to turn on him and to dump on him, and that sometimes seems to produce the desired result. He might seem to take a perverse pleasure in and negative nurturance from this response. This perhaps is a way for him to make up for the guilt he feels about his own wish to dump on others. That is, it can become a kind of species ego response—in order not to defecate on others, he ends up in a sense defecating on himself by making others do it on him. What does lower back pain have to do with all this? The pain and the muscles around the pain area are involved in the process of straining at the stool. When the client can mobilize that area he is on his way to becoming motoric and to resolving his dilemma. Everyone has some passive aggressive aspects in his personality, but those for whom passive aggression is a major character trait have to work hard and diligently to permit themselves more overt expressions that provide resolutions to their problems.

Feelings in the Thighs

The feelings in the upper thigh have often seemed to me to be accompanied by sexual or incipiently sexual feelings and behavior. Frequently a client who is seen rubbing his hands on his thighs can be understood to be about to have a conscious sexual thought or feeling. When this occurs, I watch the client carefully and listen to the verbal content if he is talking and then wonder how to introduce to him the possibility of sexual material. Of course simply telling the client that he might be feeling potentially sexual is enough to encourage sexual ideation, but often it is more easily forthcoming because there is already an inclination in that direction. Experience shows me that those clients who are having difficulty in the sexual arena, for example with sexual drives that they cannot deal with or accept, do indeed pay more attention to their thighs by stroking and rubbing them, than do clients without sexual problems.

The surprising thing is that the rubbing may easily precede any conscious feeling or thought about sexuality. The question is how much real feeling is actually there and how much do I produce by applying sexual meanings to the movement? Another question is why the feeling doesn't arise directly in the genitals and why it shows up in the thighs and hips.

I can answer this only by suggesting that sexual behavior includes the action of moving the hips forward and back and the thigh muscles, which are attached to the front of the hips, are very involved with this motion. Perhaps before the actual genital sexual feelings are involved the pre-motoric tensions are experienced in the thigh muscles.

When the action occurs, the point is to permit the further expression of the emotion overtly and consciously, and this often involves the clarification of who the target figures are. If the client is, for example, thinking or talking of his mother while he is rubbing his thighs, the therapist must reveal the underlying sexual meaning of that movement, clarify the target, and then permit the energy to flow more freely to the appropriate contemporary target. When this is done it might further develop that the loving, sexual relationship with the contemporary with whom he can move his hips and genitals freely is not sufficient to fulfill his need and wish for the mother. This can be dealt with by distinguishing the client's sexual needs from his needs for nurture and thus allowing him to express each of them more directly and therefore more satisfyingly.

Some female clients might have some inhibition about moving their hips strongly or sexually because they have been told by their parents that it was not "ladylike" to feel or move that way. The good parents in a structure might give a counter discription of that behavior, telling the client that it is normal and good that they both move that way with each other. This demonstration by the good parents can sometimes free the sexual behavior of the female client so that she can permit herself to move that way too.

Legs Apart, Legs Together
Monitoring the position of a client's legs can be instructive, for sometimes the legs are doing or saying something contradictory to what is being dealt with overtly. For instance, a

client who is in a nurturant structure with the good mother may not be curled up and in a position to take milk from the mother's breast but might be lying with her head on the mother's lap and with her legs apart. It makes one wonder if the body is not implying that the opening between the legs is where the attention should be paid. The same posture might be demonstrated by a male client, and the question then becomes whether he wants his genitals rubbed or whether he is being anally receptive. The anal receptivity shows up markedly in some structures where the client unconsciously turns his hips toward the person from whom he is ostensibly trying to get away. For instance, the male client might be recalling or re-experiencing an event where the father was being threatening, but instead of pushing the father away or running away from him the client turns his hips toward him in a seemingly receptive manner.

Sometimes a female client might be in a structure which involves her being recognized as a female sexual figure by the parents, and she may demonstrate a tendency to finger her dress or skirt while standing with her legs slightly apart. When given the opportunity to follow the movement out completely, it sometimes results in a movement often made by little girls who pick up their dresses and show everyone their belly buttons. My thought is that they are really demonstrating their little genitals for approval. This is the approach that the good parents can take in such a structure. They can respond to the client, if that is what she wishes, that indeed she is a girl, that they can see that fact and that they approve of her femininity.

The Knees

The knees call attention to themselves in two situations, when a client feels fear or the need for support. Trembling knees tend to indicate the desire to flee, collapse, or both. At the outset of a weekend workshop or at a demonstration where a new group is asked to do a species stance, there seems to be a high frequency of comments regarding feelings or tremblings in the knees. Fear in this case is a result of uncertainty about what will happen next and about how one will respond, and a concomitant wish to escape the situation. When clients are allowed to express their fear directly, some will run in place or run out of the room and some will collapse to the ground. The ones who collapse can be offered the support of the good parents and the structures can be developed from there.

There are those who feel tension about the knees but show no wish to collapse instead. They want to lock their knees strongly. This has proven to be a result of a defensive response to the need for support in some people. Rather than feel the vulnerability and dependence of support needs those individuals have learned to become extremely self-reliant and show no inclination to have anyone take care of them. Of course those individuals sometimes have a greater need for support than those who can more readily ask for help.

The Calves

Calves are not too frequently noted in my experience but sometimes seem associated with a desire to flex the foot as one does when one is stamping or digging the heel into something, much like the movement of putting out a cigarette on the ground with the heel. It seems to accompany angry feelings that result in a wish to squash somebody as well as a wish to penetrate phallically with the legs. Sometimes clients who describe tension in the calves end up doing violent jumps upon a pillow with the feet driving forcefully down on the pillow in a crushing manner.

The Feet

For some reason the toes are actively involved in both nurturant and sexual structures. When a client is doing a nursing structure, he can often be seen curling and uncurling his toes. Many people note that their feet become active in this way during sexual intercourse.

The toes at times seem to become phallic symbols as is true of any protruberance of the body. There have been structures during which the toes seemed to wish to enter or penetrate the mother for sexual reasons or in order to re-enter the womb for security.

Here I will end this sketchy tour of the body. Obviously, there is much that has been left unnoted and unsaid, but the field is enormous and needs much attention.

Writing this book has not been a logical pre-determined process. The book slowly gave birth to itself and at times even I was uncertain about what would be included. However, the twists, turns and speculations that developed in the course of writing might be instructive to the reader in showing how my ideas developed and then were applied. The end of this writing leaves me with a profound respect for the human psyche—its creativity, its capacity to survive, and its fantastic complexity.

The question foremost in my mind for the future is how to locate and describe the essence of being. There seems to be the human capacity to protect the core of being, to disguise it, hide, bury, kill it, and yet somehow secretly maintain it so that it might someday once again manifest itself even in those seemingly psychically dead and hopelessly insane. Because man can live symbolically as well as concretely, he can ascribe to various parts of his being or mind those features which are what he essentially is. It is as if the essential self is sometimes like an exiled, disguised king who is sometimes seen in one region and when the enemy forces arrive, is nowhere to be found but is rumored in some distant place. The job of psychomotor therapy and of all therapy and education, is to restore the king to the throne, openly and in contact with all the regions of his being. When the self makes an appearance in the body, it should be encouraged to remain by making it welcome and unthreatened. Then, perhaps, little by little, with both action and symbols the entire self can emerge in broad daylight and a human being, undisguised and unafraid, can be seen living himself in the world.